A
PEDIATRICIAN'S
JOURNAL

A
PEDIATRICIAN'S
JOURNAL

*Caring for Children
In a Broken Medical System*

Brian G. Orr, M.D.

B
BEAUFORT BOOKS
NEW YORK

Library of Congress Cataloging-in-Publication Data

Orr, Brian G., 1956–
A pediatrician's journal : caring for children in a
broken medical system / by Brian G. Orr.
p. cm
ISBN-13: 978-0-8253-0538-2
ISBN-10: 0-8253-0538-1
1. Orr, Brian G., 1956– 2. Pediatricians —
United States — Biography.
1. Orr, Brian G., 1956– 2. Pediatrics — United States —
Personal Narratives. I. Title.

RJ43.O78A3   2006
618.9200092—dc22   2005031719

Published in the United States by Beaufort Books
Distributed by Midpoint Trade Books
www.midpointtrade.com

2 4 6 8 10 9 7 5 3 1

PRINTED IN THE UNITED STATES OF AMERICA

For Mom and Dad
(Mary Ellen and Gerry)

ACKNOWLEDGMENTS

Thanks to Brian and Chris Stumpke for their early help with the book.

Thanks to Linda Amero for all her secretarial support.

Thanks to John Gettings for his editorial assistance in the early stages and to John McElhenny for his editorial work on the final copy.

Thanks to Pam Ashe for her belief in me and help in getting me "shaped up."

Thanks to David Nelson and Beaufort Books Inc. for giving me a voice in the publishing world.

And a special thank you to my wife, Bernadette, who for over twenty-five years has opened my eyes to worlds I would never have seen (much less understood) without her help.

CONTENTS

PART II
A BROKEN HEALTH CARE SYSTEM

PART III
EXPERIENCE IS A GREAT TEACHER

FOREWORD

My father and oldest brother were the writers in the family. When my father died, he left cases of unread writings yellowing in boxes, some of which are still in my attic. My dad's work was mostly muddy philosophical musings that only he understood, though he did manage to get one or two things published. The family favorite was the poem about a baby crying because its pacifier was stuck in its ear.

I am not a writer. I am a pediatrician. I help sick children feel better, and I help healthy ones stay that way. But I'm also forty-nine years old, and I practice during a time when doctors are questioning their profession as often as pharmaceutical companies are raising their prices. In recent years, I've read many articles about physicians changing careers. I don't want to change my career. I enjoy practicing pediatrics. But lately I've felt a need to write things down because I live an interesting life caring for kids in a broken medical system.

I have been practicing medicine for twenty-two years. I've traveled to thirty-three countries and practiced pediatrics in six of them. I've volunteered in the Dominican Republic, the Bahamas, Mexico, and Honduras, and I've studied two foreign languages — Italian and Spanish — along the way. I was a volunteer on a medical van for the homeless in Boston for six years.

Though that seems like experience enough, I have also practiced pediatrics north of Boston for sixteen years and served as chief of a pediatric department at an HMO for five. I have served on boards, spoken on television, been quoted in newspapers, written columns, and provided information for radio news reports.

Though I've managed to avoid a profession change, I have changed from working for an HMO in a medium-sized city close to Boston to a private practice in a small town farther north of Boston. I hope I have found a setting that will fulfill me until I retire.

My experiences in medicine have provided me with a treasure trove of stories. Stories of fascinating people I've met and cared for in the United States and abroad. Stories about my long and unlikely journey to becoming a doctor. Stories about what is meaningful in my life as a pediatrician. And stories about how difficult our world of medicine has become. Many people have encouraged me to tell these stories. So now I am.

To do this, I will rely on journals, letters, files,

tapes, and memories. I will share real experiences with kids, both in life and in practice. I will write about lessons I have learned in twenty-two years of pediatric experience. I chose not to use real names so as to honor and preserve the privacy of my patients. But these experiences were very real.

Whoever reads this, I hope it makes you think and stirs emotions in your heart. And I hope it brings a smile to your face.

THE BABY'S CRY

They wonder why I scream so loud
when no one is ever near.
Is it hard for them to know
the pacifier is in my ear?
If I could talk or ring a bell
that should be at my bedside here,
I'm sure they'd come a runnin' to find
that pesky pacifier in my ear.
Oh Mommy's busy, Daddy's gone
Li'l Brother is never near.
Should I call an angel to tell 'em
that horrible pacifier's in my ear?
The police and fire department would
surely respond to a scene so sincere.
I bet they'd come out just to get
that darn thing out of my ear.
And when Mommy finally comes
to comfort her miserable dear,
I'm sound asleep and couldn't care less
about that miserable thing in my ear.

Written by my father, Gerard S. Orr.

PART I

DOCTOR IN TRAINING

I

THE GUY WHO BURIED CASEY'S BALL

I was brought up in a large family. My parents were grade-school teachers and second-generation Irish Catholics. There was always a significant push to succeed in my family, which could be traced back to my grandparents, who came over from Ireland to escape poverty. This legacy was shared with all six of us kids, and each of us knew we had to do something with our lives to be successful. We were constantly reminded that we had to "pull yourself up by the bootstraps" and "do what it takes to succeed." After all, as we were constantly reminded, we couldn't live to be poor like the life our ancestors had left!

My mother pushed us the most. If she had anything to say about it, none of her six kids would be poor, and none would struggle for money the way she and her parents had done. My mother gave birth to four boys in a row and then two girls years later. We knew that my mother would probably have to hock everything just to get us through college, but we also knew that it would get done. Somehow.

My father was a good man. He tried many careers before settling on one he enjoyed. Early in life he wanted to be a doctor but he was pushed toward the priesthood. Eventually he became a policeman, though he cashed most of his paychecks as a teacher. He ended his career as a bus driver — the job he seemed to enjoy the most. My father died just after retiring. He lived his life paycheck to paycheck and barely saw the success his children would later enjoy. But that didn't faze him. He welcomed chances to tinker with our meager surroundings to improve what we had.

We lived on Long Island, New York, in a small two-story Cape. The house had gray asbestos shingles over a brick façade. One side of the house was covered with shingles down to the driveway level. We were always playing baseball. When we hit the side of the house with a ball, the shingles would chip off at the corners. The shingles were impossible to replace or fix, but how could you keep four boys from playing ball against the house? The front of the house looked good. The rest looked like a construction zone.

The chipped shingles and construction materials my dad kept around the house gave it the "never-finished" look. My dad was handy. He built the upstairs rooms, the room in the basement, and the carport. Lucky for us, he was a good carpenter, and he saved us plenty of money.

A NEW TEAM IN TOWN

My father worked hard, but he always had time to care about baseball. When the New York Mets started playing in the early 1960s, with the legendary Casey Stengel as their manager, we became instant fans. My dad had to convert from his beloved Brooklyn Dodgers, who had left town for Los Angeles a few years before. One time, we were given tickets to an autograph signing featuring Stengel and Tim Harkness, the Mets' first baseman. We four boys dressed in Mets uniforms and got our picture taken with Casey Stengel and Tim Harkness. Forty years later, I still have the photo of us with Casey on my desk at work.

We ended up receiving two balls with Casey Stengel's autograph on them. As time passed, the balls were mostly forgotten, gathering dust under beds.

That's when the story really begins.

One day we boys had lost all the baseballs we used for playing. We used a taped-up one for a while, but we used it so many times the string wound down to the cork center. A huge argument took place among my older brothers and my mother. Why couldn't she buy us a new baseball?

"Because you keep losing them and I have no spare change right now to get a ball so you will just have to make do," my mom said. That's when I suggested we use one of the balls that Casey Stengel had signed. The idea was quickly dismissed.

So I went off thinking, This is ridiculous! There are two balls in the basement that no one cares about, but we can't use even one of them for outside play! If only I could get the signature off one of the balls. So I had an idea. I found one of the balls under the couch and tried to rub off the signatures. They wouldn't rub off. Maybe if I rubbed it with dirt I could hide the signatures. So I went outside where I couldn't be seen, and rubbed dirt on the ball. The dirt left a mark but didn't cover the blue ink. I knew what I had to do. I had to bury it. A few days underground and the signatures surely wouldn't show through and the ball might look like one of our old ones. I could say I just found it! So I buried a baseball with Casey Stengel's signature on it — Casey Stengel, the future Hall of Famer.

A day or so passed and I was in the basement with my two oldest brothers. They were playing hockey on the pool table with rolled up *Sports Illustrated* magazines and the other Casey ball. At a break in the game, one of them started looking at Casey Stengel's signature. "Hey, you ever notice how Casey looped his Ss and Ls? He has good handwriting for an old guy. Let's see how he did it on the other ball. Hey Brian, get off the couch. I think I saw the other ball roll under there the other day."

Uh, oh. Oh, no.

THE NOOSE TIGHTENS

I was nine at the time, though I always acted younger than my age. I had not learned how to hide things well with my face. My brother told me to look for the ball under the couch. I looked for about a millisecond, said it wasn't there, and sat back down. "What's the matter with you?" he said. "You hardly looked. Look harder, you idiot, it must be there."

I got up, pretended to look harder, and then gave up. "I can't find it," I said. "I'm going upstairs." I wasn't halfway up the stairs when my brothers caught me. "What did you do with the other ball?" Then, "Mom!! Brian did something to one of our Casey Stengel balls and he won't tell us."

I was often my mother's favorite. I could usually get protection from her, but this time it didn't look good. I was trapped on the stairs. Before I could come up with anything my oldest brother remembered that during the argument the other day I had wanted to use the Casey Stengel balls to play outside. The noose was closing in.

"I haven't seen it for days," I said. It was a true statement but my eyes gave me away — big baby blues that can't lie. Soon the tears flowed. I couldn't hide it. I remember the parade of people — my oldest two brothers, my mother and me — walking outside. It had rained in the days since I had buried the ball. I told them I had buried the ball but had forgotten where. "You buried it?!" they hollered. "You buried one of our balls signed by Casey Stengel?!"

I was crying. My brothers dug frantically and found the ball, saw that the prized autograph was destroyed. Both stomped off with angry backward glances. Fifteen minutes later they were outside playing catch with the ball.

This is where my medical education began — in

my family. To this day, my family reminds me almost every year of this humbling experience. No matter how I succeed in medicine, in my family I am still the guy who buried Casey's ball. Of course, nobody remembers that I was trying to help everyone out by getting us a ball to play with. In life, it seems that mistakes are remembered. But in medicine, no matter how much you are trying to help, you cannot afford to make a mistake.

2

PRE-MED:
EYEGLASSES AND JOCKSTRAPS

My formal education in medicine began as a pre-medical student at Boston College. This was scary since in those days it was very difficult to get into medical school. There was stiff competition as the baby boomers jostled for an edge to get into the med schools of their choice.

I also started at a disadvantage. I had two older brothers who were at the tops of their high school classes and made it look easy the whole time. I wasn't as good a student as those two. In grade school my mother worried about how I was doing and always had to push me hard. I remember one parent-teacher conference when my kindergarten teacher tried to persuade my mother to keep me another year in kindergarten. My mother, a grade-school teacher herself, was adamant that no child of hers would be kept back.

Sister Carolis was my first-grade teacher. She wore a black habit and had eyebrows that grew thick and straight without a break across the bridge of her nose. She scowled even when she was smiling. I was intimidated and scared. She was probably not the ideal teacher for me after almost flunking kindergarten.

I cried on my way to class every day through second grade, leaving my mother, who taught in the same school, crying at the bottom of the stairs. In fourth grade, a nun finally told my mother to relax, and I would do okay. That's all I did — okay — until midway through high school. I turned it on during my last two years and gained confidence in my abilities. I loved the sciences, especially biology, and I enjoyed people, so I decided as far back as high school that I wanted to be a doctor. But did I have the brains for it? That was the question.

My brothers attended Boston College before me. They came back from their first couple of years at B.C. and tried to convince me that pre-med was too hard, that I wouldn't be able to cut it. My mother also checked in. "Are you sure that's what you want?" she said. "Well — try your best." With SAT scores of 530 in math and 440 in English, I knew I only got into Boston College on my brothers' coattails.

I still remember attending my first chemistry class. It was in a huge auditorium. The blackboard seemed thirty yards long. I sat in the third or fourth row. When the professor started writing I asked the guy next to me, "Shouldn't he be writing larger?" The guy stared at me through his glasses like I had three eyes. That's when it dawned on me why I had struck out so much during my senior year in baseball. I couldn't see far away.

Before the next class I got a pair of glasses to correct my nearsightedness. When I walked into my second chemistry class I realized that I belonged. Maybe it was the new glasses. Three-quarters of the class had similar glasses, some thicker than others. I soon heard the term "pre-med deadhead." We were the nerds of the school.

Still I had doubts. Would I be able to compete against the other nerds? Were my brothers right about it being too tough for me? Sure, I now wore glasses like everyone else, but did I really belong?

I worked hard. My worst class in the first semester was Introduction to Writing, but courses such as calculus and chemistry that were required for pre-med were actually fun for me.

Studying in the library wasn't fun. Boston College had different schools, each with its own library. Studying in the science library was frightening. All the science nerds would compete to see who could study the latest. I learned to get away and started studying at the business or law school libraries. That way I would miss out on the ridiculous competition and mind games.

I remember labs in which some students sabotaged other students' results. One group of notorious cheaters copied notes, sneaked answers to tests, and brought in crib sheets. The pre-med environment in the 1970s was cutthroat as baby boomers across the country reached the age to compete for limited medical school acceptances. Boston College was by no means alone. In fact,

B.C. was a great school. It had a very competitive rate of getting students into medical school and on the whole offered a pleasant environment for students.

Brother Jimmy

Despite the grades and extracurricular activities to fill out the résumé, it seemed like most people needed someone to supply that extra bit of pull to help them get in the right medical school. Many kids relied on their fathers or family friends who were doctors. Not I. Nope. I had Brother Jimmy. Brother Jimmy was a Jesuit Brother at Boston College who reportedly had helped several kids get into medical school. My older brothers had found out about him before I arrived at B.C. They and my mother pressured me into meeting him during my first semester.

I met Brother Jimmy at the rectory. He was short with dark, oversized black-rimmed glasses dominating his face. His lower lip protruded, rolling outwardly in a pout. He looked me up and down. "So you're the third brother in your family here," he said. "Your brothers are doing well but they're troublemakers, you know? And you won't get into medical school if you goof around like them."

He lectured me on the difficulties of getting into medical school. He told me stories of those who got in, supposedly with his help, and those who didn't because they didn't heed his words. He looked at my SAT scores and my grades so far at B.C. He told me I would have to get perfect grades to get in, and I was to check in with him every semester. Before he dismissed me he gave me one more last bit of advice.

"The most important thing is to stay away from those girls," he said. "You should wear a jockstrap when you are out so you don't get tempted by them."

There I was, a freshman pre-med student being told that it was nearly impossible to get into medical school. And, to top it all off, even if I did make it I would have to do it wearing a jockstrap! After the meeting I called my brothers. "Were you guys playing a joke or what?" I asked.

"No, he's legit," my oldest brother said. "He has gotten some people into schools. We swear."

My mother was so convinced of his legitimacy that she invited him to our house in New York during summer vacation. We all suffered through his stories about medical school applicants.

One night I saw him to his room and he took me aside to remind me about warding off women by keeping my penis protected in a jockstrap. Had he seen through my pants? Did he know I wasn't heeding his warning? I reassured him of my commitment.

Actually, I couldn't stand the guy. He was weird, and I had a feeling he was full of bull. He kept promising to introduce me to upper-crust Jesuits who would write my ticket to medical school. I kept doing my duty of popping in to see him each semester until junior year. That year I made it into the pre-med honor society. I was doing well in school without a struggle, and I had gained enough confidence to run an intramural sports program for undergraduate students. I was even confident enough to leave my jockstrap at home, despite Brother Jimmy's ominous warnings. After that I started to avoid Brother Jimmy whenever I saw his slow gait walking toward me on campus.

I got into medical school during my senior year. I was accepted at New York Medical College. It wasn't my first choice, but it was a big accomplishment. I don't know if Brother Jimmy ever found out what happened to me, but I suspect he did.

And I bet he took all the credit.

3

MEDICAL SCHOOL: TRIMMING THE WEEDS

I spent my first two years at New York Medical College on a campus in Westchester County. It was a new facility on the grounds of a hospital. There was a basic science building with two large lecture halls and lab facilities. Some people lived off-campus, but many lived in small duplex apartments across the street from the basic science building. That's where I lived for the first year. It was nice and close to school — too close.

I remember the first day of classes. A few of us knew each other from orientation, high school or college, but most knew no one and sat randomly in the big auditorium. After the first lecture, a large group of students gathered around the professor for further explanation of the material. The rest of us sat there stunned at the onslaught the professor was enduring. We wondered to ourselves, "Am I supposed to be doing that, too?"

That division of the class created on the very first day remained for the next two years. There were the ultra-intense students out to learn everything and brownnose at every chance. Then there was the group of more laid-back crammers. I was in this second group.

The environment was intense no matter which group you were in. The questions flew constantly. How hard a professor is he? Does she ask test questions from the book or lecture notes? Does he grade on a curve? Everybody was asking the same questions. Is there a surprise quiz on Friday? How many people flunked her course last year? How badly did everyone do on the test? This made for a panicky, high-strung, nail-biting, neurotic group of people.

All we did was study — even us crammers — though on Friday and Saturday nights we would relax in a bar. The nights before tests were always all-nighters. Exhausted after the tests, we would go as a group to a local restaurant to eat and drink until going home to crash.

Some smart, good-hearted people who couldn't take the pressure, quit in the first year. One guy named Jon stands out in particular. We worked out together, and Jon organized a rugby team I played on. The guy had great organizational and leadership skills. He organized games against different colleges and taught us all the game and what our roles on the team were. He was a teacher and a leader.

But one Friday Jon shocked us all. He was packing up and leaving. He just wasn't making the grade. He was failing his classes. "I just can't keep up," he said. "I'm thinking about doing something else. Maybe I'm just not cut out for it."

I believe Jon would have been a better doctor than some of those brownnoses who were cozying up to the professor after every class. Why does medical school weed out these people who seem as if they were made to care for people? A couple more classmates left in the second year. If you made it to the third year, you usually made it all the way.

To this day, I have questions about this weeding-out process and the kind of physician it creates. Why did those nice people leave medical school? Did anyone question that? Did they just accept that they weren't cut out for medicine? What happened to them once they gave up their dream of becoming a doctor?

4

MEDICAL SCHOOL:
MR. BIG FARTS

I got married and transferred to Georgetown University after my second year of medical school. At the time, my wife, Bernadette, was going to school and working in Washington D.C., and fortunately, every medical school allows for some transfers after the second year for circumstances such as mine. However, my wedding and honeymoon made me late for my first rotation, which was in Obstetric/Gynecology. When I returned, I reported to the chief of OB/GYN, who as a punishment ordered me to take two extra weeks of his course — to be made up during breaks in my schedule, of course.

Despite the rough start, I was happy I made the switch to Georgetown. After my first class lecture I felt more at home at Georgetown than I ever had in New York. Though I had made some close friends in New York, my Georgetown class as a whole was a much friendlier group. There was a class camaraderie that had been absent in New York. It seemed to be a less competitive atmosphere, with fewer brownnosing, elbow-my-way-to-the-professor-so-he-can-see-my-face-again types.

Though I felt welcome, it took a while to get used to the new environment. On the first Saturday of my third year, I made my first trip to the Georgetown campus to study. Typically, third-year medical students spend most of their time at the hospital taking clinical rotations in different specialties, but sometimes we would go to campus to study. As I was new to the school and this was my first attempt at finding the library, it should come as no surprise that I got lost.

The campus was dead quiet. There must have been a basketball game or something else that had kept everyone out late the night before. So there was nobody to ask where the library was, and my problems were multiplying. Having recently downed my morning's dose of coffee, I had to find the library — or at least a bathroom.

I popped into the campus's main building. In the hallway I met an older guy sweeping the hallway in a blue Dickies shirt and pants. Since he was the only one up working at such an early hour, I assumed he was the janitor. I quickly asked him if there was a bathroom nearby. I told him I was a new medical student and didn't know my way around yet.

"There's a bathroom right on the other side of that office," he said, pointing the way.

A partly open door revealed an office inside. I

pushed the door open and swiftly crossed the office to the bathroom on the other side. Once inside, I quickly closed the door and sat down to release a minor coffee-caused explosion.

It was then that I thought about the office I had just crossed. It was large. The desk was big and fancy. Nice pictures on the walls. An attached private bathroom. Then my attention turned to the bathroom itself. This was definitely not a students' bathroom. The fixtures were too upscale, even for Georgetown students. It dawned on me then that I better get out fast before the office's occupant returned. How could that stupid janitor direct me into this bigwig's office? Whose office was this? Would it smell after I left? It was not one of my most pleasant productions. I finished quickly and cleaned everything I touched as fast as I could, just like my mother had taught me. I peeked out the door and saw that the office was still empty. Good. Yes, this was a big, fancy office all right — nice paintings, diplomas, signed pictures of important people. OK. I'm outta here.

Out in the hallway I came across the stupid janitor once again. I wasn't mad. No harm had been done since I hadn't gotten caught in there. In fact, maybe the janitor would clean up and spray the bathroom before Mr. Bigwig got back. I thanked him.

"You're welcome. Where are you from? " he said.

We started to chat. I told him I was from New York and had just transferred into my third year at the medical school. I was about to cut things short and ask where the library was when he asked another question.

"Where did you do your undergraduate work?" he said.

I thought to myself, "Come on, Buddy. I just want to go to the library. And why are you so curious?" But I was polite, remembering that he had just helped me out in a pinch. "I went to Boston College," I said.

Needless to say, I wasn't expecting the response I got.

"Oh, Father Monan is a good friend of mine, and he has done such a good job up there," the janitor said.

He was unlike any janitor I had ever met before. How was he "good friends" with the president of Boston College? It occurred to me then that this guy must be some kind of high-ranking maintenance man or something.

"I'm sorry, I didn't get your name," I said.

"Oh, I'm Father Healy. I'm the president of this institution," he said. "And what is your name?"

I can't imagine how shocked I must have looked. I wish I could have seen myself. I was either all red or all white. "Just call me 'Mr. Big Farts,'" I thought.

I eventually got my name out. All of a sudden, I had all day to chat. Forget the library, I had to gab with President Healy for a while, at least until the smell in his bathroom dissipated. He continued before I could say anything else.

"Well, if you're ever up at the reunion at B.C. and run into Father Monan say 'Hi' from me," he said. "The library is out this door to your right, but if you're looking for the medical school library follow the path around to our left. Nice chatting with you."

"Thanks, Father Healy," I managed to say. " Nice chatting with you, too."

So much for keeping him engaged in conversation. Knowing what awaited Father Healy in his office, my only resort was to get out of there immediately and stay up near the medical school part of campus for the next two years.

It was a memorable start to my third year of medical school. This was to be the year that my classmates and I would learn about seeing and managing patients for the first time. But before I had seen my first patient that year, I had already learned an important lesson thanks to the president of the university: don't judge people by their looks.

5

MEDICAL SCHOOL: DIAGNOSIS — FEAR

My third year of medical school was fun. We were finally out of the classroom and into the hospital. We were being taught how to examine people, take their histories, and evaluate their cases. You can tell a third-year medical student by his eagerness. When talking about cases during the third year, students would bring up the most esoteric diagnosis first because they were just learning about these obscure diseases in class. They wouldn't think of the more common illness — and the more likely explanation — until later.

We spent six weeks at a time in different clinical "rotations." The typical ones for third year were Internal Medicine, Pediatrics, OB-GYN, Psychiatry, General Surgery, and Orthopedics. The "weeding out" process was over, but there was still competition among the students for entry into residencies, which are the three- to five-year programs after medical school. The best students got the best recommendations to the best residencies in the country. Only a few elite students in the class took part in this competition. The rest of us were just trying to struggle through each rotation.

Our job as students was to tag along after the interns and residents, trying to pick up educational pointers along the way while helping them do the "scut" work. Scut work meant obtaining blood, urine, and stool specimens from patients, getting them to the lab, and then chasing down the results. Fortunately, as students our scut work was limited to our own patients, and we were assigned many fewer than the interns and residents. So we usually had more time to spend reading, looking up articles, or talking with our patients.

Many third-year students would acquire illnesses they read about. At least, they acquired them in their minds. Many a third-year student had to be told that Rocky Mountain spotted fever is a tick-borne disease not often seen in Washington, D.C. Or, that they weren't the right age or gender for gallstones. Or, that a particular cancer only occurs in people over sixty.

My fourth year of medical school was even more fun. Besides one more rotation each in Internal Medicine and Surgery, we took elective courses most of the year. That meant we could actually do a rotation in an area that interested us, and do it at a hospital where we might want to work after graduation. Many of the rotations were in subspecialties, so a student could explore areas of potential career interest.

By March of my fourth year, selections for residencies were made based on the rotations you had done and the interviews you had had. In an annual tradition, every medical student in the country was matched with an internship somewhere in the country. I was part of the Military Match, since I went to medical school on a military scholarship. My parents had helped pay our college bills but paying for post-graduate education was up to us. I was assigned to Bethesda Naval Hospital, which was my first choice. After Match Day, all fourth-year students knew where they were going next, so the rest of the year through graduation in May was a breeze.

THE STUDENT BECOMES A DOCTOR

At the end of my fourth year, I heard of a hospital in Virginia near D.C., which offered moonlighting jobs for fourth-year students. Even though we hadn't graduated, the hospital allowed us to work 24-hour shifts and be paid as interns. Being short on cash, many of us took advantage of this opportunity. I did only once.

I went to the hospital on the night I was assigned, and the outgoing intern handed me my beeper and gave me the "sign out." That's the term used in medicine for the turn-of-shift meeting about the patients for whom you are responsible. Fortunately for me, I was covering a weekend and there weren't many patients for me to watch. I got a few calls, but only one that I remember well.

I was called to see an older man who was having trouble breathing. When I walked into the room, the nurse told the patient, "The doctor is here." That was the first time anybody had referred to me as "the doctor." It struck me as odd, since I had always been called a student to that point in my career. It was a signal that my carefree student existence was coming too quickly to an end.

I said hello and listened to the man's breath sounds. He was wheezing. I looked at his chart and had no idea what to do. Here I was, "the doctor," but I didn't know what to do! I asked the nurse about his medications and she told me he had just been taken off theophylline. I recognized that as an asthma medicine. "All we have to do is put him back on that," I said. I wrote the order for the nurse to give him that medicine, and that was it. I was very relieved. In my first time playing "the doctor," I had considered the problem and come up with a solution. "I can do this," I thought.

After meeting my wife for dinner, I went back to see the old man. He was feeling better and I felt even more relieved. I went to find the nurse. "So the medicine worked," I said. She shook her head. "No, we called the attending physician who then ordered epinephrine. The medicine you ordered would only work over several hours, and he needed something right away."

Later, when I threw my cap into the air at graduation, I knew I had earned an "M.D." after my name. But I also knew that there was plenty I didn't know about being a doctor. Certain expectations go along with the "M.D." title in our society. People speak to you as if you know everything about every illness.

Nurses tell patients, "Your doctor is here." One Catholic man told me that he equated doctors with priests.

My internship was only four weeks away, and I wasn't sure I could I do it. I was scared. The responsibility of actually being a doctor was so great. Even after earning the title, after all the education, there was still so much to learn about caring for patients.

6

BAHAMAS:
THE WISDOM OF DR. JUDY

I took many rotations during my fourth year at Georgetown Medical School, but one stood out from the rest because of the professor who taught it. The rotation was in the Bahamas, but it was hardly run out of picturesque thatched roofed huts on the beach. "Dr. Judy" ran the clinic for Bahamian children in the slums of Nassau, the capital city. This was the invisible Nassau, out of sight of the luxury hotels and sparkling blue waters. Dr. Judy was loved by all the kids in Nassau, and there was little wonder why. She was gentle, sincere, and loving to all the kids and their families. Her clinic was located amid tin-roofed huts with no running water or electricity. Fortunately, the clinic itself had relatively modern facilities, including a small laboratory. Dr. Judy surrounded herself with a very sweet staff of Bahamian women and teenage students.

The medical students from Georgetown would come down for six-week rotations. We stayed in small rooms in church-owned housing on the grounds of a local church, and we rode our bikes through the slums to get to Dr. Judy's clinic. Many times kids would run after the bikes and yell "Dr. Judy, Dr. Judy!" For them "Dr. Judy" meant doctor. She was the only doctor they had ever known.

Dr. Judy was a great teacher. She knew I was interested in pediatrics so she took me under her wing, showing me simple things about examining kids like how to hold them or how to distract them. She taught me about listening to the sounds of their heart and lungs. She was wonderful. I remember how she would invite us over for dinner and to take a dip in her pool. The pool was her favorite place to give lectures in pediatrics. There in the cooling waters, I listened to some of the best pediatric lectures I have ever heard.

The rotation was memorable for another reason. While all of Dr. Judy's staff were warm and welcoming, I particularly enjoyed one bright teenage boy who was the lab technician. He was friendly and always spent extra time teaching me things in the lab. Dr. Judy thought that one day she would lose him to the U.S. The boy and I became good friends.

One day the boy and I rode our bikes to Paradise Island, an island full of beaches and resorts and attached to Nassau by a bridge. Once there we cruised around and looked for a beach. All the beaches were private and restricted to hotel guests, so we got off our bikes and locked them in a grove of palm trees to search for a hotel beach on foot. We found one hotel beach, so I told my friend to walk like he belonged there and we'd have no problems. We walked onto the beach and soon found ourselves in a volleyball game. We were having a great time until my friend got nervous and abruptly took off on his bike. I ran after him but he told me he needed to go.

The next day at work I asked him why he had left so suddenly. He told me that the waiters and hotel staff were signaling him to leave the beach because it was not acceptable for black Bahamians to be seen at a white people's hotel nor on their beaches.

As a white foreigner, I could go anywhere on the island, but a smart native Bahamian could not do the same simply because he was black. I loved my pediatrics rotation with Dr. Judy but learning about the privilege of my own skin color was the biggest lesson I learned in the Bahamas.

7

MIRACLES

My first serious case as a pediatric intern was a case of meningitis while I was working at the Naval Hospital in Bethesda, Maryland. I picked up the phone and the voice on the other end said, "You better come down and help us out. There's a sick baby down here." When I reached the emergency room there were people hovering around a six-month-old baby. The baby was limp and ashen gray, but as soon as we tried to move her, she groaned. Meningitis patients suffer great pain in their spinal cord when moved and will fight to keep from bending to avoid that pain. The six-month-old on our table was no different. When we tried to bend her head forward so her chin went toward her chest, she tried to keep her back and neck straight and her body came off the table as if on a board. We knew what we had to do. The baby needed a sepsis work-up, and fast.

A sepsis work-up is an evaluation of body fluids including urine, blood, and spinal fluid to find out if an infection is present. The fluids are drawn and sent to the lab for chemical analysis and culturing, a process by which they are warmed in an incubator to quickly grow any present bacteria for easy identification. While incubation of the cultures takes a few days, the initial chemical and cellular analysis takes less than an hour and can give you clues as to whether an infection is present.

I talked to the baby's mother and explained what we were going to do. She was crying. I had to ask her to wait out in the waiting room while we performed our gruesome tasks. We drew the blood from the arm, which is not so bad. We placed a catheter to get urine, again not so bad. Then we rolled the baby over to her side for a spinal tap, passing a needle into her back between her two lower vertebrae. Usually when you roll a baby over to its side the child flexes easily into a balled-up position that allows easy passage of the needle. And usually the spinal fluid is clear when it passes from the needle to our clear test tubes.

When I did the spinal tap, the baby did not flex easily and the fluid came out cloudy. In healthy patients, spinal fluid is as clear as water, but in those with meningitis, the fluid is clouded by white cells trying to fight infection in the lining around the brain and spinal cord. With this baby, you couldn't see through the spinal fluid at all. I exchanged glances with the other doctors, and in those glances we all agreed this one was serious. There was a silence in the room, as everyone concentrated on the work at hand. I felt ill deep between my heart and stomach because I knew this kid had bad meningitis.

We used to do hundreds of spinal taps a year. Concern about meningitis was the most common reason for admitting children to the hospital while I was in training. Most of those admissions were done as a precaution. The children were given three days of antibiotics while we waited for the cultures to incubate, and if the cultures came back negative we sent the child home. Today, due to newer vaccines that have greatly reduced meningitis among infants, pediatricians see many fewer cases of the disease and can be more judicious about who needs spinal taps or full sepsis workups.

But back in the ER in 1983, we were seeing real, life-threatening meningitis at full force. On this child we started the antibiotics and moved the baby to the intensive care unit. We then realized somebody had to talk to the mother. Who wanted that unpleasant task? What could you say? What were the right things to tell her? No way I wanted to do that.

That's what I was thinking, but this is what I said: "Sure."

So I and my truthful, easy-to-see-through baby blues and baby face went to comfort the crying mother whose child had the worst case of meningitis I had ever seen. In the waiting room, the mother was there with her mother and father. I introduced myself and brought them to an area where we could talk. We stood in a corner of the emergency room. If we sat it would appear too ominous. I recapped what we had done with the sepsis work-up. Then I told them that we thought she had meningitis, but we had already started fighting the infection with antibiotics.

"But isn't it quite serious?" the mother asked.

"Yes it is," I said.

"Will she die?" she asked. All of them were crying.

"We are giving her the antibiotics and will have her in the ICU," I said. " I certainly hope she will not die."

They were quiet. I asked if they wanted to come to the ICU to see her. When we got off the elevator at the ICU the staff told me she wasn't settled yet and we would have to wait. Just then I got paged and had to go to another floor. I told the family the staff would let them into the ICU, and that I would stop in to see them again. The mother turned as I was about to go and looked into my eyes. "Will she be okay?"

I looked back into her eyes and said, "Yes, she's going to be okay."

I don't know if I was trying to believe it or if I was lying to get away. I didn't have a good feeling, but I hoped I had said the right things to keep the family's hope alive so they could support their little girl.

A few days later the baby was doing better than expected. I stopped in when I could, but I had plenty of other patients to see so I wasn't around much. After a week, the baby was awake and responding well. In time, she was transferred from the Intensive Care Unit to the regular ward. I bumped into the mother shortly before her little girl was discharged.

"She's going home and she only has mild hearing

loss," the mother said. "She's going to be OK, just like you said. I just wanted to give you this."

She gave me a postcard-sized plastic sign that read "Believe in Miracles." We parted with a hug. I was touched that this mother felt that my contribution to her child's care warranted this gift. I wondered if she gave it to me because she thought I believed in miracles or because she thought I should have more faith in miracles. Had she seen the doubt in my eyes about what would happen to her child? Or had she received from me the faith she needed to support her baby? I want to believe the reassurance I gave her that night gave her the faith she needed. Twenty-two years later, that sign remains on my desk. After twenty-two years, I still believe in miracles.

8

INTERNSHIP: A LOST YEAR

The first year of training after medical school is called an "internship." After the internship year comes the "residency" years. The number of years of residency required to complete your training depends on your specialty: three years for internal medicine, three years for pediatrics, five for surgery, etc. As you'll have guessed by now, I did my residency in pediatrics.

During my internship we were on call every third night for most of the year. Sometimes we'd be on call every other night. While on call we stayed nights at the hospital and were responsible for the ward, the nursery, labor and delivery, and the emergency room. I recall my internship year in a blur:

Another IV to start and a sepsis work-up to do. A C-section soon. The ER called. Another admission. Will I get sleep? I got three hours sleep — great night! Fall asleep at dinner. Another night on call. Call comes up fast and goes slow. Always thinking about sleep. Did the IV get started? Did you get to the labs? The IV. The IV. Sleep. Sleep. Will I get sleep? The ward called. IV needed. The nursery. 28-weeker needs a blood gas. C-section, bad baby, intubate, to NIC-U, lots of work, guaranteed to keep me up. Sleep, when? ER called. Labor and Delivery. Nursery. All fires out, sneak some sleep. They call again. I give an answer. They call back. Was I sure of that answer or was I still asleep? Off call. Great. Some sleep before dinner. No, at dinner! No life. No relationships. Commiserate with colleagues. Party at times. On call again. Did I get the labs? IV started. Another sepsis work-up. Another spinal tap. Should we use that medicine? Get the results. Need to present the case. Morning report. All the attendings. The chief. Do your presentation, get criticized, defend yourself, more criticism, justify yourself. This is how to learn—

At home one time during internship, I fell asleep after I sat on my bed and pulled my pants down to my ankles. Another time I was sleeping as my landlord showed the condo in which we were living to a potential buyer. "Oh, go ahead in. He won't wake up," my wife, Bernadette, said.

Looking back, I realize my internship was a lost year. I have no memory of any event that took place outside the hospital. I vaguely knew who was president. My wife tells me about events I attended with her that year that I don't recall at all. One thing I do know is I was good at inserting IVs, drawing blood, and giving spinal taps.

After the year of internship the Navy sent me overseas to Italy. I had received training for several weeks in each specialty — OB-GYN, emergency room, and substance abuse. Those rotations along with my pediatric training were supposed to prepare me for my overseas assignment.

At the time, I was greatly relieved to get out of the hospital and go overseas to start my tour of duty. I was going to practice in a small island clinic serving many women and their children. I thought it was going to be a great experience. Looking back, it's clear I had no idea about the experience awaiting me.

9

DIABETIC

The Naval Hospital in Bethesda is responsible for caring for many of Washington's embassy personnel. While interning there I had the opportunity to learn about other cultures and meet people from around the globe.

I happened to be in the clinic one day when a young Brazilian couple brought in their six-year-old boy because he was peeing a lot. They thought he had some sort of minor infection. They were not expecting a big diagnosis like diabetes.

During my examination I found that the boy had sugar in his urine — a lot of sugar. While normal blood sugar hovers around 100, his was over 500. Child diabetics have an inactive pancreas that decreases the output of insulin. Insulin helps move sugars into cells and helps initiate the sugar's metabolism within those cells.

Without insulin, sugars stay in the bloodstream. The kidney, which ordinarily keeps sugars in the bloodstream and out of the urine, gets overloaded with sugar and spills it into the urine. Therefore, diabetes is a simple discovery for a physician. One sample of urine and — voilà — you have an answer.

But I was an intern, on the lowest rung of the ladder among doctors. I knew little to nothing about many pediatric issues or how to manage them, including diabetes.

To the family from Brazil, however, I was a genius. I had immediately discovered what the problem was, and I was about to take action. I admitted the boy to the hospital, where a competent group of doctors would teach the parents to care for their diabetic child.

I remember the mother cried when I first told her about the diabetes. After some reassurance that he could be cared for and do well, she felt better and was ready to go to work and care for him. The family learned eagerly in the hospital. The father and mother were equally involved at the hospital, and they took their boy home after about three days.

For the better part of a year, I took care of their son's diabetes in outpatient visits, where I mostly saw him with his mother. Diabetes is often simply cared for in the first year. Many diabetics go through a "honeymoon" period when they need little insulin to manage their sugar. I rarely had questions on his treatment, and when I did I went for advice to our endocrinologist, a diabetes expert.

When the time came for him to return to Brazil, the

boy's whole family joined him for the last visit. They were overly grateful for the actual work I did. We took pictures together and they gave me a small gift. It was an onyx elephant, which is the Brazilian symbol of good luck. They told me I was always welcome at their home in Brazil.

I still keep the elephant on my desk more than twenty years later. It certainly was a symbol of good luck because — lucky for me — they never knew how little I knew about diabetes at that time. And I was lucky to experience their genuine gratitude.

10

THE ECTOPIC LEUKEMIC

During my internship and residency I took care of many patients with leukemia. At the Naval Hospital we had a wonderful oncologist named Richard who was gentle, kind, and very smart. His personality and subtle French accent made him beloved and respected by patients and staff.

Since all of Richard's patients had to be admitted to the ward for their chemotherapy treatments, we got to know them well. Often we knew their parents and immediate family on a first-name basis. It was as if Richard and the interns and residents involved with their cases became extended family during their life-threatening struggles. Everyone on the house staff had a story about patients like these, stories about those who survived despite harrowing medical experiences, and stories about those who did not.

I remember one lovely teenage girl who had recovered from her leukemia a few years earlier but returned one evening with extreme pallor. Her parents and the staff assumed her cancer was back and admitted her immediately. But the diagnosis wasn't so straightforward. In patients with leukemia, white blood cell production becomes so numerous that it overwhelms and reduces red blood cell production, which causes a shortage of red blood cells. This shortage of red blood cells is known as anemia. With this patient, her red blood cell count was very low, but her white blood cell count was normal. This was a job for Richard. He, too, was worried about a recurrence of her cancer so he took her to his office for a bone marrow examination. He looked under the microscope and found no leukemia.

Then what was the problem? Richard spoke to her and she revealed that she had had sex for the first time the previous month and her period was a little late This was something she only confessed to Richard, and it gave us some much needed direction. We did a pregnancy test but it was negative. Richard was convinced, however, that she had an ectopic pregnancy.

An ectopic pregnancy is a pregnancy in the fallopian tube that is very dangerous because it is prone to hemorrhage. If it is missed, the patient can die from blood loss. Richard asked the house staff to get a gynecological consultation, a pretty routine step, but as luck would have it the doctor on call for consults was our least favorite OB-GYN doctor. He was a chief resident who thought he knew everything. Unfortunately, our hands were tied. We had no choice but to call him for the consult.

The arrogant resident arrived at our ward and began criticizing everything we had done.

Why were we consulting OB-GYN when the pregnancy test was negative?

How could there be an ectopic pregnancy with a negative pregnancy test?

Why didn't the patient have pain?

Why is your attending doctor looking for odd things like an ectopic pregnancy?

The resident ended by concluding that Richard the oncologist must be wrong. "Of course she has a recurrence of her leukemia," he said. "If she has an ectopic I'll eat my scrubs!"

After the resident did a quick gynecological exam, the girl complained to us that he had hurt her. She said he had been really brisk and seemed to just want to get the exam over with. The resident told us the exam was negative and there was no ectopic pregnancy.

We dutifully reported this to Richard, our attending doctor. In the hospital hierarchy, "attending doctors" are the fully certified physicians who oversee interns and residents and are in charge of a specialty. Richard was the attending in charge of pediatric oncology. After the resident's brisk examination of the girl, he was not happy to say the least. "This is bullshit," Richard said in his French accent, "Get another consult." in his French accent. "Get another consult."

We told Richard that was impossible. "This guy will have a tantrum," we told him. "We already worked at resident level. It's time for you to talk, attending to attending."

Richard didn't have a strong case for ectopic pregnancy. After all, the pregnancy test was negative, and it should have been positive if there were a pregnancy, even an ectopic one. Our patient showed no signs of bleeding, and she had had sex only once. Her period was not that late. The arrogant chief resident — who despite his bad attitude, was trained in OB — said she had a "normal exam." But Richard had a feeling. He knew he was right. Richard was sure that the blood smears were clear of a recurrence of leukemia. He knew the girl's pallor and low blood count were caused by blood loss, and with no visible blood loss it had to be internal blood loss. That could only mean she was pregnant.

Richard went to an OB colleague he trusted to present his case. He asked his friend for a favor: supercede the chief resident and do his own consult. So the OB doctor came up to the ward with the chief resident in tow. I could tell the chief resident was very angry and was just dying to tell us "I told you so," but with one of his bosses present he was well-behaved. While they examined the girl and performed an ultrasound, we prepared the chief resident's scrub suit on a platter in a back office.

Minutes later the OB doctor and the chief resident both ran out of the exam room to the operating room. The girl was about to undergo emergency surgery to remove her — you guessed it — ectopic pregnancy.

We learned a great lesson that day from our friend

Richard: follow your feeling as well as the facts. That feeling in your gut may very well save a life.

And, oh yeah, we didn't do anything with the scrubs. That joke was just for us.

II

LA REPUBLICA DOMINICANA

When I finished my internship at Bethesda Naval Hospital in July 1983, it was the Navy's policy to break up the three-year residency program by sending doctors on a two-year medical assignment before resuming their specialty training.

Before I began my two-year assignment, I volunteered to work for a month in the Dominican Republic. This was the second time in two years I'd worked in a poorer country — remember my stay with Dr. Judy in the Bahamas the year before. My time in La Republica Dominicana would greatly influence my later interest in international volunteer programs.

Georgetown University sponsored the program in which dental, medical, and nursing students teamed with faculty for a four-week rotation. We set up clinics in four different rural communities of the D.R. for one week at a time. Many of the people we treated had never seen a doctor or a dentist before our arrival — and may not have seen one since. The need was tremendous, and what we learned was indescribable.

We were welcomed to each town by the town leaders and a group of townspeople. The welcomes were so warm that they made the long bus trips worthwhile. During our stay, these same people let us live in their houses. They gave up their humble beds and small wood shacks with dirt floors so we would have places to sleep. Like them, we bathed in the river, about a three-quarter mile walk from town, and we ate the food they cooked for us.

The school building was usually the best building in the town, so we would set up our clinic there. Each morning a long line of people snaked outside our clinic before we could even finish our breakfast.

We treated many health issues. Headaches, colds, dizziness, and back pain were all common. Many people raised a laundry list of physical complaints they had had for a year or longer. When we asked how long someone's back had been bothering them it wasn't unusual to hear them say, "Oh, for years. I'm a very hard worker, you know." I guess they figured since this was the only doctor they would be seeing for the foreseeable future, they better get all their questions answered. Many of the problems and their treatments were repetitive and monotonous — Tylenol for headaches, antacids for indigestion.

Often, though, it wasn't possible to offer a long-term solution to a particular health problem. For example, when farmers come to you with back pain from endless hours of the bending and lifting needed to run their small farm, how can you tell them to change their lifestyle to get rid of their pain for good? Many of the women we saw struggled with back pain. Well, let's think about this. Most of them carried heavy loads of goods to market on their heads every day. Back pain? Why not? "Hey, you should get a truck and drive it down to the market and back," we could say. Sure.

These were not "lazy" poor people, as many Americans crammed into their Lay-Z-Boys might think. More often these were hardworking poor people, and you could tell it when you shook their hands. Their skin was thick, hard, calloused and strong. The women's handshakes could bring you to your knees. Like their fathers, husbands, and sons, they had strong, hard, muscular hands chiseled by the hard labor they did to keep their families fed.

During our time in the Dominican Republic, we knew we were there more for our own experience than for their treatment. After all, wouldn't their maladies return once they ran out of our "magical" medicines? But many of us wanted to think about how much of a medical impact our trip would have. What kind of positive physical outcome would result from our visit? What could we go home to the United States and say we did to treat these friendly Dominican people? As I learned on this and other volunteer trips, you have to measure your impact with that one special case.

The most dramatic case I saw in the D.R. was a four-year-old girl with a horrible eye infection. This was before the hemophilus influenza vaccine — not that a new vaccine would have reached these children on the Dominican border with Haiti. Hemophilus influenza (H.Flu) is a family of bacteria that causes meningitis, ear infections, and pneumonia in young kids. It also causes periorbital cellulitis, a severe eye infection that makes pus drain from the eyes. The infection if untreated can spread to the brain. This is the infection this four-year-old girl had. In the U.S. these infections have been drastically reduced in the last ten to fifteen years due to an amazing new vaccine, but in 1983, H. Flu was still a dangerous pathogen.

The girl had a swelling covering both eyes. The eyelids were red and her eyes were oozing pus. There was no way to see if her inner eye was infected. I would only be able to diagnose that after lifting her eyelids, but her eyes were too swollen to do that. If her eyes were not moving correctly that meant the infection was deeper behind the eyes and could lead to more serious consequences such as meningitis.

A CAT scan would have helped us see if the girl's infection had traveled deeper. A CAT scan stands for Computerized Axial Tomography. It uses powerful X-rays to examine inside a person's skull or other parts of the body. But of course a CAT scan wasn't available to us. This girl's eyes were so red-hot, swollen, and pus-filled that I had no doubt invasive H. Flu disease was present. This was not a simple case of conjunctivitis. In the U.S. at that time, the girl would have been admitted to the hospital for days and intravenously fed a steady diet of bacteria-killing antibiotics. But we were secluded in the mountains of the D.R. with only a handful of donated antibiotics at our disposal.

Time was of the essence because we were leaving the next day for another town several miles away. Before long, the entire staff was wrapped up in this little girl's case. While I was putting her on two antibiotics that were on hand — Keflex and Sulfacetamide — the nurses were helping the mother to guide the girl around, as she was essentially blind at that point. Meanwhile, our translators were trying to arrange a follow-up visit. We were all suffering from a hopeless feeling that our very limited resources would prevent us from successfully treating such a dramatic infection. The consequences for the little girl would be serious. If it spread internally she could die.

The following week the girl came walking into our clinic. She and her mother had walked five miles to see us. The girl's eyes were still red, but less swollen. They were now opened a crack and there was no pus. Our mood was exuberant. We now had hope. We gave the mother enough medicine for three weeks.

After we got back to the U.S., someone sent us a picture of the little girl. Her eyes were open and she was fine. A case like this reminds us of our impact. Today that girl would be blind, or dead, if we had not been there to help.

Our time in the D.R. allowed us to share ourselves with the lovely Dominican people, and they shared themselves with us. We gave them hope and recognition, while they gave us lessons in hospitality, joy, hard work, and determination.

On the day we left they threw us a party. Americans and Dominicans danced and drank and enjoyed one another. Most of us Americans spoke little Spanish, but somehow we got our feelings across as we did the meringue and celebrated our shared experience.

12

ROLLER COASTER

After my four-week volunteer stint in the Dominican Republic, I went to Italy as part of my two-year military requirement. I was assigned to a small clinic on an isolated island in the Mediterranean Sea called La Maddalena. To get there, one had to fly to Rome, then ferry or fly to the island of Sardinia, then drive an hour north to another ferry that would take you on a twenty-minute ride to the island of La Maddalena. There, on an island about five miles in diameter, was a small fishing town, a submarine base, and about 2,000 U.S. Navy families.

During the summer, the island and the entire archipelago were as beautiful as any Mediterranean seaside community. The water was a gorgeous, clear aquamarine, and sailboats dotted the horizon all day long. The beaches were populated with topless women. It was an idyllic summer location.

The winter, however, was gray. The sky, the clouds, the sea, the rocks. Everything. Even the wind was gray.

At that time, Italy had laws restricting home heating, and the government determined the dates and hours you were allowed heat based on where you lived. In our zone, heat was allowed only eight hours a day. That's not much when you consider that these islands sat in open water where blustery winter winds shot off the water and cut through everything. For six months, the year-round inhabitants huddled around space heaters in their otherwise cold, drafty homes because it was the only heat available for most of the day.

The services on La Maddalena were different from those in the U.S. There was no mall, no self-service, and no fast food. In fact, there wasn't anything fast about the Italian markets. But the Italian community was warm and welcoming to those who were daring enough to venture out and experience it.

Most American servicemen and their families were not adventurous enough to try and be part of the Italian scene. Many didn't want anything to do with shopping for fresh foods in the open-air markets. They were appalled at the way meats were left hanging naked in butcher shop windows. They didn't want to try local vegetables or delicacies.

Instead, most Americans chose to live isolated amidst the American community. They only shopped at the small American stores on the base, and they only ate at the fast-food joints on the base. And though a few brave souls would venture out for Friday night pizza or pasta, it amazed me how many people lived through two years of such isolation. They missed out on many great experiences.

An Italian Adventure

Though I hadn't traveled much at that point, my past experiences had taught me two things. First, I recognized how important it was to take time to appreciate and be interested in the communities and culture I was visiting. Second, it's always very early on in your exploring that you run headlong into the eye-opening differences between your own culture and another.

A few days after my arrival, I had to buy a washing machine. My wife, who is better at languages than I am, was still in the Dominican Republic, so I went alone to visit Italian stores for the first time.

Near the port of La Maddalena was a small downtown lined with stores. There was one store for bread. One for meats. One for fabric. One for fishing gear. Many for shoes. Some for women's clothes. Some for men's clothes. And, of course, an appliance store. The stores were by no means roomy. Usually, they were no more than one street-level room for the shop with the shopkeeper's apartment directly above.

At the appliance store, there were several items on display but there wasn't a large selection. There seemed to be one of everything: one washer, one dryer, one stove. I did my best impression of browsing considering I couldn't understand anything on the tags. I picked one washer quickly. That tends to happen when the only factor you care about is cost, and you're searching for the cheapest one.

I stood near my selection, as if on guard, so nobody else would take it from under my nose. The salesman was a short, older man with a gruff demeanor. I remember wondering if maybe he didn't like serving Americans. I gestured to him that I wanted to buy the machine I was guarding. He muttered something, went behind his counter, grabbed some keys and headed for the door. At the door he motioned to me with his hand. His hand was held out with the back of his hand toward me, his fingers toward the ground and his wrist limp. He moved his hand toward me and back toward himself as if shooing away a cat. It was Saturday and nearing noon. Most stores would be closing for the weekend soon, not to reopen until Monday morning. I thought his signal meant it was lunchtime. In other words, "Go away. I'm outta here. Come back some other day."

But the old man kept flicking his hand toward me and saying *Venga, venga,* each time louder than before. Startled and confused, I backed up. He was by the back door and I was slowly backing away from him further into the store. Did he want me to watch the store while he ate lunch and had a siesta?

He disappeared completely out the door. A few seconds later he popped his head back in. Venga! he yelled. And once again the back of his hand told me, "Shoo."

I thought then that he didn't want me to buy anything and I should just go. So I followed him out the back door. As I left I caught a glimpse of him walking away. A second later he reappeared, sticking his hand around the corner of the building.

Venga!

It finally dawned on me that he wanted me to follow. So I did. He took me to his mini-truck, which had a cab, flatbed, and three wheels, but was about the size of a Volkswagen Bug. The cab had little room for a second person, but he motioned for me to get in. (Perhaps he was taking me to lunch?) I squeezed in. Each time he shifted gears he hit me in the knee. It seemed like we were driving up and down the hills and in and out of traffic, all at knee level. No seat belts. Horn honking. It was get-outta-my-way driving, and size — or our serious lack of it — didn't matter. I don't think I blinked the entire ride. I had no idea where I was going, what his intention was, how long this would take, or whether I would survive to tell anyone about it.

The ride probably took all of three minutes, but when you're new to a place, don't know your way around, and are riding in a three-wheeled truck at bumper level to every other car on the road, time passes frame by frame.

At last the shopkeeper took an abrupt turn and stomped on the brake pedal. The truck lurched forward and we skidded to a halt just feet from a house. I assumed it was his house. (Maybe lunch was at his place!) My knees wobbled a bit as I got out. He was in a forklift at the corner of the house before I had straightened up. I turned and saw a giant stack of washers and dryers in cardboard boxes, six to eight high. He picked a box off the top and plopped it on the flatbed. In a second we were back in the truck almost cheek to cheek, smelling each other's breath. We zipped back to the store as fast as we had come. My new washer teetered in the back on every turn.

"*Dove?*" (pronounced DOE-vay) he said. "Where your house?" he translated in poorly spoken English.

I lived in the upstairs apartment rented from an Italian man named Secci. "Signor Secci's," I said.

He knew instantly. It was a small town. "*Si, si, Signor Secci, vaben.*"

In a minute we were at my apartment. He set up the washer. In another minute, we were back at his store, which had been left wide open the entire time.

"*Grazie,*" I said. Thank you. He shook my hand and was off to his next customer.

"Never in America," I thought to myself as I walked to my car, proud that I had smoothly acquired the needed washing machine. Venturing into the Italian community would be a breeze after that.

It was fascinating to me that most Americans at the base on La Maddalena wanted no part of the Italian experience. I don't know if it was fear or arrogance. But to me, experiencing another country and its culture taught me a lot about my own.

13

THE ISLAND OF NAVY MISFITS

Navy work life revolved around the chain of command. Work gets done by following the orders of your boss. Period. Job descriptions are clearly written: "Do what your boss says." This wasn't always true in medical circles, however.

The Navy considers doctors a different breed. But we are necessary, so they tend to overlook our lack of discipline. For instance, doctors are horrible about knowing whom to salute and who should salute them. I decided early on to salute everyone in a "Hey, how are ya today?" style.

Also, doctors require a degree of privacy and independence in their work, so officers can't command a doctor to treat a patient a certain way. I say "a degree of privacy" because not everything was private in the Navy. Patients' health records, for example, were Navy property. Nevertheless, life on the base at La Maddalena, like any other base, for the most part followed the whims of the commanding officers and the interpretations of those whims by those lower on the chain of command.

We were in Italy at a time of increased attention to terrorism, not long after terrorists hijacked a TWA flight from Athens to Rome and suicide bombs struck the U.S. Marine barracks in Beirut. This was the time of President Ronald Reagan and Communist paranoia. On our island base, we were told to avoid kidnapping by terrorists by varying our routines, taking different routes to work, and wearing different clothes.

The problem was we lived on a circular island. So what were we to do, go around the island clockwise one day and counterclockwise the next? Would that fool the terrorists? Could we outsmart them by wearing a white shirt one day and a red one the next? Who were we kidding? We Americans stuck out in this small Italian town no matter what we did. But that didn't stop the higher-ups from sending down reminders practically every day to vary our routines.

From what I've heard from doctor-friends who spent time on other Navy bases, this sub base in Italy was unique. The chain of command was disorganized and the action on the base followed suit. The submarines and their crews were under the Atlantic Submarine Fleet Command, but the boat that subs tied to for repairs was under the Mediterranean Fleet Command. The land support base was under the European Support Command, but the branch clinic I worked in was under the command of the U.S. Navy Hospital at Naples, Italy. As a result, there were four captains from four different commands vying for control of one small island base. The result was chaos. It's no wonder La Maddalena was known in Navy circles as "La Mad."

I learned later that this base was often a dead-end assignment for captains and other Navy personnel. The prime jobs that led to promotions were the destroyer and aircraft carrier assignments. In the Navy, being assigned to a land base or submarine tender — the sub repair boat — gets you nowhere.

For a pediatrician in-the-making, however, La Mad was a great choice. It was a much better experience than working with Navy servicemen on a ship. At the sub base I would spend the majority of my time caring for the women and children family members of the Navy servicemen. Little did I know, however, that the trade-off for choosing this isolated base was that I was accepting assignment on an island of Navy misfits.

ASSIGNMENT ANTIBUSE

Let's start with the captain in charge of the land support base. He had been exiled to this remote island to finish his career. It was well known that it was his last assignment. He would not be promoted beyond his captain's rank. It was also widely known that he had blown other commands because he was an alcoholic. (There was little that could be kept secret very long on La Mad). The captain was often seen drunk at parties and had a small group of people who worked to keep him from hurting himself or others. The interesting thing was that our medical office had the dubious assignment of delivering an Antibuse tablet to him every morning.

As the newest and lowest ranking of the two MDs on the island, I was given this responsibility. Everyday on the way to work I would visit the captain to give him his Antibuse pill, which is used in the treatment of rehabilitating alcoholics. It is designed to make them ill if they drink while on the medication.

Since it was well-known that this captain was frequently drunk, the medicine was either not working or he wasn't taking it. When I delivered the pill, the captain would take it from me and chat with me a moment. Sometimes he would turn around and appear to swallow the medicine and drink some water. Often he would dismiss me prior to taking it. When I reported this to my senior officer he said that I should play along since the captain would be retiring soon.

Another captain was a chaplain — a Catholic priest who ran the Americans' only Roman Catholic parish on the island. He was the second-highest ranking officer at the base, but he really belonged to his own command of chaplains in the Mediterranean.

Several women came to me and said the priest had had dinner with them and then fondled them when he got them to a private place. Two women were severely shaken by the event, which I recognized because I was their doctor. I reported the events to the priest's commanding officer in Naples. His commanding officer came to our island and heard the priest's confession. He told me that this was his solution, and the problem was solved.

Not on this tiny island.

The number of people in the priest's parish shrank as word got around the island. Though I kept the issues in confidence, the women did not. Once they told one other person about the priest, there was no way to keep things confidential. Turnout for Sunday Masses fell, while the Protestant services grew in size as rebelling Catholics became Protestant.

I could go on and on about the Navy's island of misfits, but one story especially stands out.

THE EXCITABLE XO

The executive officer (the XO) was a commander who would never reach the rank of captain. He had a panicky streak and was sent to La Mad for what appeared to be his last assignment. The Navy hoped he would retire after La Mad. However, he took his job seriously and had little recognition of his own ineptitude. He dreamed of getting his career back on track, and since the captain was a drunkard, the XO felt this small island was the perfect setting for him to show his superiors that he was in charge.

One weekend day when I was on duty I received a call from the XO.

"Get down to my office and bring some Valium, quick!" he said. "There's a woman going nuts down here. She's stripping off her clothes and attacking my people."

Obviously, this was an extremely bizarre situation. I went and got the Valium, though I was doubtful I would need it. I went down to the XO's office and walked into the lobby. There, sitting by herself, was a woman in civilian clothes. I had seen her a couple of times in the clinic because her boss had ordered me to test her for drug use. She had tested positive and was on continuous observation for repeat offenses. She was sitting at the front desk of the lobby with her feet up, smoking a cigarette. It was clear she wasn't the person usually assigned to greet visitors to the Commanding Officer or Executive Officer. I guessed by her defiant position that she was in trouble again.

I sat on the corner of the desk and asked her what was happening. Before she could answer, I heard a screaming, tantruming XO through the door. The woman said she had been accused again of drug use, and the officers wanted to court-martial her and send her back to the States.

"They wanted me to change into my uniform to be court-martialed since you have to be in uniform. I said 'no,'" the woman said. "They were trying to force me to change. I pushed this girl away, got back into my civilian clothes, and came out here. The XO has been screaming since."

That was the most reasonable explanation I would get. I told her the XO had asked me to bring Valium for someone who was attacking his people. "You can give me that Valium to help me forget this place," she said.

She obviously knew her drugs well.

I told her she looked too relaxed to need the Valium, and I knocked on the door. The XO's ranting and raving didn't stop when I walked in. He was purple at this point. His lawyer, a reasonable guy I knew well, was on the brunt end of both the ranting and the raving. The lawyer had a family and was happy to be at a land base with them. Many people in the Navy spent time at sea separated from their families. We often confided in each other about the insanity of the place. He leaned over to me and joked, "Did you bring the Valium, and can you give him a shot real quick?"

By this time several chief petty officers and support staff were hovering around the room, trying to calm the XO or stay out of his way. "We can't have this! We can't have this druggie attacking my people!" he was yelling. "This is an outrage! We have to get her court-martialed and get her out of here and to Naples."

The XO finally noticed me. "Thank goodness you're here, Doc. Did you bring the Valium?" he said.

Everyone in the Navy called the doctors "Doc." It just goes to show the separate nature of doctors. I was never recognized by my rank like the other lieutenants, just simply "Doc."

I told the XO I had the Valium but didn't think it was a good idea to give it to a drug addict if he still had a case to make against her. "Besides, she just told me she wants it," I said.

All of a sudden there was a sober look on his face. He asked what should be done.

"I think you should get her to Naples — even in

civilian clothes," I said. "Let them deal with her off the island."

"Good idea. That way I don't have to deal with this lunatic," he said before ordering the MPs to take the woman away.

The lawyer and I walked out and went for a cappuccino at a bar. He, too, loved the Italian community and spoke Italian almost fluently. "Congratulations. You have now been fully initiated into the lunacy of this island," he said. "If it wasn't for those of us who keep our heads and really run things around here—"

So that was the situation. Lunatics running the asylum on an island of Navy misfits. But that was only the beginning.

14

THE SANE MINORITY

It was a wild ride both administratively and clinically at La Maddalena. The cases were surprisingly unusual, but that followed suit from the unusual disorganization of the base itself. Perhaps a more experienced doctor wouldn't have been surprised by the cases, but remember, I began the adventure after just a one-year pediatric internship that had included one rotation each in OB, ER, and drug abuse. I was just one year out of medical school.

Late one Friday night when I was on call, a woman was brought into the clinic with burns and bleeding from the scalp. Friday night was usually the party night for the Navy personnel — a typical payday ritual. And I suspected that had something to do with the woman's visit to the clinic.

She had recently arrived on the island with her husband. Typically, after arriving on the island families stayed in hotels until another family left for the States. The military housing was that tight. I'm sure the Italians helped keep it that way so the base would remain small. Nonetheless, it was common for people who just arrived to stay in hotels for weeks before settling into military housing.

On this night, the woman's husband was on duty on the ship. Friends persuaded her to go out with them for dinner and drinks. Around midnight she decided to walk back to her hotel. A drunk sailor saw her at the bar and followed her. He knew her husband and knew he was on duty. He persuaded her to let him into her room. He proceeded to rape her and then in a panic set the bed on fire, hoping to kill her. But she tried to get away. He stopped her and pulled out a samurai sword (yes, a samurai sword), chopped her in the head several times and left her for dead in her smoldering hotel room.

She regained consciousness and staggered out into the streets until she was picked up by the Navy police. The man was arrested. He would later be sent to the Navy brig for many years.

As I sutured the many cuts on her scalp, I asked the woman whether she was sure it had been a samurai sword. Here on an isolated island in the Mediterranean, where would he have gotten a samurai sword? "Oh yes, it was a samurai sword," she told me. "They're sold in the Navy ship's store."

Violence in Navy families was common. Our clinic set up a local child abuse committee called the Family Advocacy Committee. It was made up of two psychologists, a Navy administrator, a social worker, and myself. We reviewed abuse cases and made recommendations to the Navy administration about whether these families should stay or be sent back to the States. Of course any family that was returned from an overseas assignment could kiss their Navy career goodbye.

This brought to our attention a huge problem. The medical profession's definition of abuse was much different than the Navy administration's definition of abuse. This ugly fact was never so apparent as in the cases when someone important was found to be abusive.

A Boy, Bruised

One case involved a Chief Petty Officer (CPO). CPOs are the highest-ranking enlisted members. The enlisted ranks were not officers. They were people who signed up for the Navy without a college degree. The CPOs are the top of the bottom and often serve as right-hand men to the top-ranking officers.

One day the wife of this CPO brought her son to me to check his face and eyes. His mother calmly explained to me that the boy had had an altercation with his father after speaking back to him. His father had slapped him hard, leaving a bruise in the shape of a hand across the left side of the young man's face. One part of the bruise handprint was close to the boy's eye. The eye also had a slight bruise on the conjunctiva, the clear lining that covers the white part of the eye.

The mother explained all of it as if it were normal in the household. The boy seemed unabashed. They were here in my office solely to make sure his eye was OK. When I brought up the issue of abuse, they were both defensive. Mother and son both said the boy had deserved it.

The next day I received a call from the school. The boy's teacher and principal wanted to know if I was aware of the bruise on his face. They suspected it was abuse, but they wanted to know what I thought. I brought the case up to our Family Advocacy Committee. The psychologists and social worker agreed with me. We filed our report to the ship's captain. The report said his right-hand man — his CPO — had abused his son.

The captain called me after seeing the report. He said he knew his CPO very well and knew him to be a dedicated family man. He was not a child abuser. Bothered by that report and our findings in other reports, the captain attacked my work on the committee.

"What are you running over there, some kind of witch hunt?" he said. "You've been picking on some of my good men. I want this to stop or I'll have to call the captain at the Naval Hospital to look into this committee of yours."

Shortly afterwards my wife and I were out to dinner downtown. The downtown on this island was as small as the Navy community it hosted. Before we could finish scanning the first page of our menus, we heard a loud American man talking in the corner behind us.

"Frank, do I look like a child abuser?" the man said. He was angry and slurring his words. "Can you believe that doctor accused me of child abuse?"

It was my friend, the CPO. He and his buddy were drunk, getting louder and more obnoxious every minute. At one point he yelled over to me, "Hi, Doc. Are we bothering you?"

The waiter came to our table and asked my wife and me in Italian whether he should get rid of them. We thought it would be best, and the waiter obliged.

Sure. That captain knew his man. Watching and listening to this drunk in the restaurant was all the evidence I needed. I could tell he was a true family man. I only hope he didn't go home and hit his wife and kids again that night.

Our committee learned to be more selective about who were reported to the captains. We tried to work with the families undercover, hoping to resolve their cases before they reached the committee. We heard many families' stories, and it got to the point where I could, if I wanted to, go down the street in La Mad and tell my wife who was sleeping with whom and who was abusing whom.

One man, a father of six, worked for the shore captain (the one on Antibuse) at the land base. He was the captain's personal secretary. He and his wife hosted many single men after they arrived from the U.S. and before they settled into military housing. After suspecting that rumors of sexual impropriety about them had made their way around, the thirty-five-year-old wife paid me a visit. I suppose she was fearful of her case being turned over to my committee.

I had seen her in the office often but always with one of her kids. This time she was alone. She tearfully confessed to me that on many occasions her husband had asked her to give blow jobs to the single men who stayed with them. She didn't know what to do and didn't mind doing it so she went along with the favor.

Her confession was completely out of the blue for me. I had not heard any of the rumors. She didn't think she did any harm but she was concerned because she didn't know what I had heard or what the committee would say. She feared being sent home. I reassured her that the committee would not even hear about the case.

Cases like those certainly stay in your mind. At the time, I was working a busy clinic, seeing as many as forty patients a day. All of a sudden, I'm faced with a mother of six who is confessing to giving blow jobs to single enlisted men on their arrival on the island. Amazing. Welcome to La Mad.

I wish it were a joke. But the events were anything but. Women and children were hurt regularly, but the Navy brass didn't care. And my small Family Advocacy Committee could do so little. I hope I had some impact on the safety of a few of those families. I'll never know for sure if I did. It was very frustrating and scary to be in that position. The most disturbing thing was that I was part of a small group on the island that thought this violent and unusual behavior was abnormal. That was the crazy thing about those cases and being on La Mad. We were the minority.

15

THE MOTHER
AND BABY DOCTOR

I was ill-prepared for obstetric work since my only background in it was a one-month OB rotation during my internship. Yet I was now one of two doctors on this lonely, isolated, crazy island handling all the gynecological and prenatal OB cases.

Every woman on the island in a Navy family had to choose my colleague Henry or me for their care. Henry had an administrative role as lieutenant commander in charge of the branch clinic, which didn't leave him much time for clinical work. In fact, he avoided it, preferring to play "captain" with all the others. He spent his time hopping around from meeting to meeting, wanting only to further his Navy career.

I saw most of the patients and became known as the friendly doctor who took care of the families. Eventually, most people preferred seeing me over

Henry, even though Henry had more experience. He also had more training in OB-GYN. I had more in pediatrics. Originally, our complementing backgrounds seemed to be good for the clinic, until Henry fell in love with his administrative work.

The women liked coming to me because I talked to them openly and listened to their concerns. They appreciated that I treated them for who they were, not merely the spouse of a Navy man. One woman, who may have felt a little *too* comfortable, came to the clinic during lunch one day. The doors of the clinic were closed and locked while the staff ate lunch on the third floor.

"Doc, I know you're in there! I need to see you!" she yelled. Up in the lunchroom on the third floor, the whole staff could hear her. "I have an itch — you know — an itch down there!"

I recognized the voice. She was a repeat customer and quite a character. I had come to like her because she was definitely on the wild side and not "Navy" at all. She wasn't just another sit-at-home obedient Navy spouse.

We thought she would go away if nobody responded. Our clinic was set between the homes of Italian families, and although we knew they couldn't understand her, we felt embarrassed for her.

"Doctor!" she yelled in a singsong voice. "I have an itch and I need to see you!"

I went out on the balcony. "Hi, Melinda. You know, we're open in a half-hour."

"Yes, but I needed to come now! You don't understand! I have a really bad itch down there," she yelled while repeatedly pointing to her crotch. "I can't stand it anymore!"

At this point, the noise of her drama had called all the lunching Italians in the neighborhood to their windows. I couldn't help but wonder if they thought this was some twisted performance of *Romeo and Juliet*, but in reverse.

I decided it would be better to get her off the street before she pointed at her crotch a few more times. I examined her and gave her the medicine for her "itch."

Although OB-GYN wasn't my specialty, I became very comfortable with it over time. I learned how to insert IUDs. I took care of infections. And I handled prenatal care up until the women were close to delivery. When they were near term, it was clinic procedure to send the mothers to a hospital in Naples so they could await their baby in a setting better equipped for labor and delivery.

During this time I learned to look for signs that the mother or baby was at risk. I became good at knowing when someone needed to see the OB doctor in Naples. And while my later cases were fairly routine, in the beginning not everything went smoothly.

In one of my early cases I saw a woman who brought her husband along because she was afraid to go through the gynecological exam on her own. She had some discomfort in her vaginal area and was concerned about an infection. Usually we used a nurse as an assistant (and witness) during a vaginal exam, but in this case, the couple insisted that the husband stay for the exam so a nurse wouldn't be necessary. I permitted their arrangement and asked the husband to stand close to his wife and reassure her during the exam.

I took pains to explain everything I was doing or was about to do. I always tried to be gentle on GYN exams after hearing from my wife what it was like to go through one. Nonetheless, many times the exam was painful when infections or other problems existed. Such was the case with this woman.

In the middle of the pelvic exam, with my hands between her legs, my index finger and middle finger touching her cervix, she had severe pain and screamed. At her screams, the reassuring husband turned white and fainted. He fell like a tree. As he fell, he hit a screen which slid until it hit the door. He landed on his head with a thud.

The woman tried to sit up to see what had happened to her husband. I encouraged her to lie back down since my fingers were still inside her pinned to the exam table.

She screamed again. Not in pain this time, since my fingers couldn't reach her cervix in this position, but from the sight of her husband on the ground. Staff from the check-in area downstairs and from the lab came and knocked on the door.

"Is everything okay in there, Doc?"

So what's the correct answer to that? I couldn't possibly let anyone come in and see this half-naked woman with my hand stuck between her legs and her husband out cold on the floor. Word would be around the island in a second.

"Everything is fine," I said. "We just had a small

accident." As I spoke my hand and wrist were strained by the woman's desire to keep watch over her fallen husband.

Did he have a heart attack? Did he just faint? He looked awfully pale on the floor. The staff outside the door didn't seem confident of my answer. Was it my tone? They tried to push their way in, but fortunately or unfortunately — I'm not sure which — they couldn't get in because the screen was wedged between the door and my desk. They could only open the door an inch. Even if I needed help they couldn't have gotten in.

After what seemed like several minutes, I persuaded the woman to lie back down. She was crying hysterically with her forearm over her eyes. After extricating my hand and rubbing my wrist, I went over and slapped the husband lightly. He woke up and I helped him to a chair. I put the screen back in place and covered the woman up.

I peeked out the door and told everyone to go back to work. Everything was fine. The husband apologized and the woman finished getting dressed and sat next to him. She apologized, too. I apologized to them, and we laughed about it. I prescribed some medicine and told her she should come back in two weeks to be rechecked — this time without her husband!

Trouble for Linda

Another OB patient I had was definitely not the typical Navy wife. We once saw her get a henna tattoo on her pregnant belly at a beach party. Linda was young, perhaps twenty-one or twenty-two years old. She liked me personally, but she never followed my instructions or kept regular appointments with me. Towards the end of her pregnancy she ran into trouble.

I knew she was near term and was supposed to be seeing me weekly, but I hadn't seen her for a couple of weeks. The last time I saw her we talked about her going to Naples to wait out her pregnancy, so I assumed that she had gone there.

While boarding a bus with my wife for a weekend tour, who did I see but Linda getting on the same bus? She was finally going to the hospital in Naples.

"Hey, what are you doing here?" I asked her. "I thought you went to Naples weeks ago."

Linda said she had decided to hang out in La Mad instead of going to Naples. But now that she was headed to the hospital, she wasn't sure if she would make it since the contractions had already begun. "Doc, I hope you're going to Naples," she said. " I might need you on the flight."

As luck would have it, my wife, Bernadette, and I were taking a tour out of Naples and were booked on the same flight. I told Linda we should check her before getting on the plane to see how far along she was.

When we got to the airport I suggested that she and I linger in the back of the bus after everyone else got off. After seeing her blow through contractions for the hour-long bus ride I thought it was important to know if she could make the flight to Naples without giving birth. I did not want to deliver a baby — with my little experience — on an airplane.

Everyone got off the bus and while they searched for their luggage, Linda slipped off her underwear, straddled a bus seat and threw her legs over the back of two seats. I examined her and discovered she was leaking fluid. I asked her how long that had been happening. She said it had been a couple of weeks.

"Why didn't you call me?" I said.

She didn't realize how serious the situation was. "I knew you would send me to Naples and I wasn't ready yet," she said. Unfortunately, Linda didn't know that leaking amniotic fluid for so long would affect her baby. She was still only two centimeters dilated, and it was a short flight, so I made a quick decision.

"Let's go for it and get you to the hospital," I said.

When we arrived at the hospital, Linda was whisked away by the OB team. We said hurried good-byes and she disappeared. At least she was in safe hands.

When we returned from our trip, we called the hospital and found out that Linda's baby was very sick. He had been put on a respirator immediately after birth even though he was full-term, and had been medically evacuated to a U.S. military hospital in Germany that had a neonatal intensive care unit.

It turned out that because of the amniotic fluid leak, Linda's baby boy was born with hypoplastic, or underdeveloped, lungs. He required many months of respiratory care. He had chronic lung problems that required supplemental oxygen for years. He would spend his first six years in and out of hospitals.

Years later our paths crossed during my residency

when we were both reassigned to the Washington, D.C. area. I took care of Linda's boy and his bouts with pneumonia many times during my residency. Though she and I spoke many times, we never discussed the plane flight and my decision to have her go to Naples. But had she delivered her sick baby on that flight there would have been no equipment to keep him alive. He would have needed a respirator immediately, as he did before and during his flight to Germany. Even though he had a rough several years, he might not have made it at all if he didn't make it to Naples. We were lucky to get past that flight — and we both knew it.

A Broken Friendship

I encountered two other serious cases that hit home personally. I had a friend on the island with whom I played racquetball every week. We had great competitions. He was the assistant to the lawyer with whom I also became friendly. The lawyer and his assistant were more reasonable than most on the island.

The assistant's wife came to see me and we discovered she was pregnant. I followed the pregnancy and for the first fourteen weeks things went fine. Then over the next several weeks we became concerned that she wasn't growing anymore. During one particular visit I became very concerned because we had a hard time finding the baby's heartbeat. I felt she needed an ultrasound.

In the years before I came to La Maddalena women would have to fly to Naples to have an ultrasound. They would get up at five-thirty A.M., ferry to the main island, drive an hour south, fly in a military cargo plane to Naples sitting in netting instead of a seat, drive from the airport to the Naval Hospital in Naples, have the ultrasound, and reverse the trip.

I thought this was ridiculous since I had discovered an Italian OB doctor on La Mad who did his own ultrasounds. For fifty dollars the woman could save herself the long, tiresome trip. When given the option, the women overwhelmingly paid the fifty dollars and stayed local for their ultrasound. Over time the Italian OB and I developed a good professional relationship, and he would help me out as a local consultant on many cases. Many times he was more helpful than the Navy OB Docs in Naples who were distant — literally and clinically.

My racquetball friend and his wife came with me one day to see the Italian OB. We chitchatted as we walked down the street. None of us thought anything was wrong. After explaining the situation to him, the doctor directed my patient to a table where she lay down for the ultrasound.

We all watched the screen as anatomical parts came into view. I explained what the doctor was describing to me in Italian.

"Here's the leg— Here's the head—"

But then there was a long silence. I kept talking to my friend and his wife about the machine and the technology, while the Italian doctor tried to catch my eye. I eventually caught on and shut my mouth. The doctor's look told me something was seriously wrong.

"E morto," he said. It's dead.

My friends asked, "What? What's wrong?"

"The baby is dead," I said.

"Are you sure?" they asked, starting to cry. I asked the doctor in Italian, and he said he was sure, showing me the tiny heart that was perfectly still.

As I walked with them back to my office I explained what I thought had happened and what still needed to be done. She had had an intrauterine demise, or the death of the baby in the womb, at nineteen weeks gestation. I answered their questions, reassuring them that I was sure it was nothing they had done. I also had to explain that in order to get the baby out, they would have to induce a delivery. That induction couldn't be done in Naples. Instead, they would have to fly to Germany to have it done.

After they returned from Germany I saw them once. I could tell they were still hurting. There was still a mourning process they would have to go through. There were no more racquetball games. The friendly competition was gone, and it appeared the friendship was broken. The hurt was too much for my friend.

I often wonder if during a stage of their mourning — the anger stage — some anger was directed toward me. Intrauterine deaths are almost always naturally caused. Nothing in prenatal care can prevent them. Prenatal care can only discover them and make sure that the fetal tissue is removed from the uterus before there is infection or other complications. I don't know if they ever had kids. They left the island six months later. We never spoke again.

Another devastating OB case involved a twenty-five-year-old woman who was excited about her first pregnancy. She and her husband wanted kids very badly, and when I confirmed her positive test it was remarkably fun to see someone so joyful over her first pregnancy.

After a few visits it was apparent that her uterine growth rate was far below normal. There was no audible fetal heartbeat at this point, but it was still early. I consulted a doctor in Naples who told me to give her a second pregnancy test. Her test was still positive.

A few weeks passed and her fundus, the top of her uterus, was not increasing in distance from her pubic bone. I consulted the OB in Naples again. He suggested that I order a quantitative HCG. This was a test that would measure how much HCG hormone the pregnancy was producing. This is the hormone that is tested in pregnancy tests to tell if someone is pregnant. What he was asking me to do was quantify how positive her pregnancy test was. This would show us if the level of the hormone was appropriate for the age of the pregnancy. If it were low, it would mean the pregnancy was likely to be aborting.

To our surprise the test revealed that her HCG level was tremendously high. When I told my OB colleague he said he suspected she had a molar pregnancy. A molar pregnancy is essentially a tumor of pregnancy. It is rare. There is no fetus — just a tumor. The tumor can be removed from the uterus, but if it gets a foothold into the uterine lining itself then a hysterectomy is necessary. And that would mean that she would never bear children.

It did turn out to be a molar pregnancy. The woman went to Naples and had the malignancy successfully removed without a hysterectomy, but for the next two years she could not get pregnant. Every month she needed to get a pregnancy test to see if the tumor had recurred. If it did, she would have to get a hysterectomy. I saw her for her monthly tests, and she was very discouraged about her dream of ever having children. The excited young woman who had come to my office a few months before was now battling to maintain her fertility and her life.

She left the island before her monitoring time was over. When she was leaving I copied her records for her, and we said an emotional goodbye.

Unlike most of my OB cases, I was fortunate enough to see this story's resolution. Years later when I was at another naval hospital in the Midwest the same woman came into my clinic. There was a moment of recognition followed by hugs. Not only was she healthy and happy again, but she was also the mother of two children, whom she happily introduced.

I have not practiced OB-GYN since living in La Mad. I didn't expect to have such an emotional experience practicing it for those two years. Since then I have had many complex cases in pediatrics, and I have forged many strong relationships with parents. But I won't forget the intensity of the relationships I formed taking care of those women and their pregnancies.

16

EMERGENCY

On La Mad occasionally we had to use our "ambulance," an old Fiat, to pick up emergency patients. Every day, the corpsmen would review the emergency equipment on the aged machine. They would also start it up, if they could. It was usually a fifty-fifty proposition. They would take it for a spin around the block just to "run the engine a little." On the way back up the cobblestone hill to our clinic it would often stall out. So they would leave it there for the day and let it rest until the next time.

All four tires on it were bald and they ballooned out sideways like no other tires I have seen before or since. If they were Goodyears, they were more likely to be made out of blimp material than rubber. As the ambulance rode, the cabin bounced on the tires. Imagine the ride on the cobblestone streets. I kept telling the chiefs we would be safer picking up emergencies in our own cars rather than that silly Blimpmobile. Nevertheless, probably due to Navy regulations, if there was an emergency involving Navy personnel the ambulance was required to do its job and pick up the patient. Several emergencies stand out in my memory.

One day we got a call from the grade school that one of the children had suddenly gone blind on the playground. The corpsmen were salivating at the chance to take out their Blimpmobile, and they sped away. The school was no more than ten minutes away, on the other side of the island in a Navy family residential community. I continued to see patients until the corpsmen returned two hours later with a little blond boy. We guided the boy into the small "emergency room," which was actually just a room across from the check-in desk that was equipped for emergencies. The boy walked with his arms straight out in front of him and his eyes wide open.

I mentioned to the corpsmen that it had taken a long time to get him. They said they had stalled several times trying to get up the hill. They finally gave up and walked, leading the blind boy on foot. The image of the boy walking up the hill on cobblestones, arms outstretched, with corpsmen on either side of him, stayed with me for a while. This is not the usual approach to an emergency room.

When I walked into our emergency room the ten-year-old boy was being helped up onto the table. He sat staring straight ahead. His mother sat crying on a chair in the corner. The school nurse was wide-eyed with worry. "He really can't see," one of the corpsmen whispered as I entered.

When I stood in front of the boy he seemed to look right through me. I introduced myself and asked him what happened. "This big kid threw sand in my eyes," the boy said. He believed that the sand had made him go blind.

"I see," I replied. Looking back, I guess that was a poor choice of words.

I took an otoscope (for ears) and ophthalmoscope (for eyes) off the wall and spoke to him again.

"Here, could you hold this?" I said. He immediately grabbed the ophthalmoscope as I looked in his ears. He had grabbed it without a second thought.

This showed me he could see, and the problem was he had convinced himself he couldn't. I did a brief exam and then had him lie down with the lights dimmed. I brought his mother out of the room and quietly told her he was having a hysterical reaction to the bully's attack. He could see. She looked relieved and stopped crying. She had seen my trick and knew I was right. However, I told her we would have to treat him with seriousness for him to believe he could see again.

"I'm going to put some powerful eye drops in your eyes to make you see again," I told the boy, dropping some harmless saltwater drops into his eyes.

He rested in the dimly lit room while I went back to seeing other patients. When I returned, he told me he could see a little but things were still fuzzy.

"We can use the powerful drops one more time,"

I said, "but if they don't work this time we'll have to do something a bit harder."

After ten more minutes he was ready to go. He really appreciated me saving his vision. He was adorable — the poor kid. I didn't see the need to correct any of his notions. In my mind as well as his, he had lost his vision and I had restored it. I hope the bully swallowed hard in the principal's office before receiving his punishment.

No Petty Success

One New Year's Eve, someone called to say there had been an accident. One of the Chief Petty Officers decided to drive his car through a telephone pole. Yes, I do mean through it. The pole was cut in two, the top half dangling from the wires while the bottom half was splintered over the smashed hood and windshield.

When I arrived at the clinic the CPO was surrounded by other drunken petty officers. The victim hadn't been wearing a seat belt at the time of the accident, and he had cuts on his face and arms. A flap of skin that had once covered his knee was flipped up to his mid-thigh. I sewed up his wounds and X-rayed him from head to knee. Moments later, when he stood up and moaned, we X-rayed his ankle as well. He had a fractured collarbone, fractured ribs, and a fractured ankle. We slung his arms, splinted his ribs, and cast his ankle. After hours of work he was sobered and sore.

Our nurse, who lived next to him, agreed to keep

an eye on him after we sent him home. The next day she called me and said he looked pale. I visited the CPO at his home and not only did he look pale but his blood pressure was low. In caring for his multiple wounds and fractures, in my inexperience I had neglected his internal wounds, particularly his spleen.

At this point I was sure it had ruptured as a result of his rib fractures. This was dangerous and a time-sensitive condition because he could bleed to death. We called the medical evacuation plane and got him to Naples. My only worry was, had I delayed too long? Was it now too late?

I sweated this one out. I worried he would die of internal wounds because I delayed getting him to Naples by twelve hours. I went on vacation two days later, but I couldn't relax because I worried about the chief. I called the clinic from Munich, Germany and they told me he had had his spleen removed and received blood transfusions, but he was going to be okay.

When I returned from vacation, the CPO community treated me like a hero. In the Navy, their acceptance could make your life much easier. I appreciated it, though I often think how I could have been vilified had he not made it because of my oversight.

Sudden Death

The two emergencies on La Mad that hurt me most occurred just months apart in my second year. Both involved babies.

One day before work I was called urgently to the

clinic. A mother that morning had found her three-month-old baby not breathing in his crib. I rushed in to find the mother leaning over her little boy. He still wasn't breathing.

The corpsman and I brought the baby into the emergency room. The mother followed. There was no heartbeat, no breath, and no signs of life. There was nothing to do.

I knew both the mother and the baby because I had been caring for the baby since birth. The mother wasn't that young, perhaps in her mid-20s, but this was her first baby. She had been very caring toward her baby and was a happy mother.

"He's dead. I'm sorry," I said.

I wrapped the baby in his blankets and had the mother sit in a chair holding him. She cried. We cried. I don't recall the father being there until later because he was on duty on the ship when it happened. I gave them lots of time with the baby. It's important to bond with babies at their birth, but it's equally important to bond with them at their death.

Bonding with death answers a lot of "what ifs" that could come up later in the mourning process. Parents think things or ask questions that may not seem rational but make perfect sense at a time of such grief. "Maybe my child really isn't dead — maybe he's still alive and is being adopted by some other family," they might think. Or, "Maybe the doctor took my baby and it was his fault he died." When parents are so depressed, they can get very "unreal" about their baby's death.

It was tough to witness, but it felt right. I knew we were doing the right thing in allowing them time with the baby. We just needed to be there for the parents. There was nothing to say. Eventually we took care of the body and made the appropriate arrangements. As is procedure after such a devastating event in an isolated place, the family was rapidly sent home to the States.

A few months later, a woman came to the clinic with her baby completely wrapped up. It was difficult for the nurse to find out what the problem was and what the woman wanted.

"This woman wants to see you for the baby but she is being strange about it," the nurse told me. "I think it's a feeding problem but — good luck."

In the exam room, I asked the mother how I could help. She slowly unwrapped the baby and I began to see an ashen, immobile, stiff-faced baby appear out of the blankets. I moved over to take the baby. "I think my baby is dead," she whispered to me as I took her child. The mother was stunned.

I listened for heart sounds. There were none.

I listened for lung sounds. None.

The baby was already stiff and there appeared to be old milk in the baby's mouth. The mother said she had awakened at six in the morning to feed the baby. She fed the baby and they both went back to sleep.

"Then when I woke up, I found the baby like this," she said.

I agreed with her that her baby was dead. Her husband had gone to work early, so we called him to the clinic. The parents and I went through a process that was all-too similar to the one I had endured a few months before.

Two cases of Sudden Infant Death Syndrome in three months were startling for a small island community. I spent a lot of time over the next few months squelching rumors and dispelling myths. Some people wondered whether the Italian food or water was to blame, while others wondered about toxins from the Navy ship. The whole Navy community seemed to mourn for these two innocent babies.

There are few things in life as tough as witnessing a child's death. The younger the child the harder it is. The mourning process is long, and when a baby has died it is almost impossible to truly get over it. No parent believes their child should die before they do.

By the time I left La Mad, I was no longer green. I had more training than a residency in the United States could ever provide. I had treated severe medical and psychological issues with little support from mentors or peers. And when it was time to go, I was ready.

17

ARRIVEDERCI

For the rest of my two years at La Mad I continued to be the main clinician, seeing most of the patients who walked in the door. I would see forty to fifty patients a day while my colleague Henry kept brownnosing the captains and upper ranks in hopes of furthering his career. Unfortunately, he didn't last past the first year.

I went home to the States midway through my time in La Mad to attend my brother's wedding. I was back in the U.S. getting dressed for the ceremony when I got a call from the charge nurse of the clinic. It seemed that Henry had lost it. In my absence he had had to do all the clinical work by himself, and seeing those forty to fifty patients each day by himself had gotten to him. Something snapped. He went nuts. Literally.

Henry was taken from the island and sent to Naples in a straitjacket. I told the nurse, "I'm going to get off the phone and go to my brother's wedding. Let's make believe that you never reached me. Because when I come back, as I understand it, I will be working that clinic by myself for the next year." The nurse agreed. He told the command in Naples I was unreachable and they would have to send a temporary replacement.

When I returned to La Mad the naval hospital wanted to send Henry back to me. "What for?" I said. "He can't practice in this small place now. Nobody will see him anyway."

I didn't back down. All I needed was to be dealing with a nutcase who also happened to be my superior. They eventually agreed and sent Henry back to the States. After he left, the naval hospital in Naples periodically sent physician's assistants out to our island to help me. I continued to share call with two doctors from the ship, but for the most part I was on my own for that second year — running the clinic on the island solo.

Though mostly tied to the pier helping submarines, occasionally the sub-tender ship would go to sea for thirty-six hours just to run the engines and do drills. One afternoon I got a call that I was needed on the ship. I was told the ship was heading back to port because there was an emergency. I immediately left the clinic and many waiting patients and was taken to a waiting military police speedboat.

We raced out towards the ship. The seas were rough. We bounced like crazy until we pulled alongside. The crew dropped the netting so our corpsman could climb aboard. One of the ship's doctors came out, and a corpsman scurried up the netting and grabbed an envelope. The corpsman passed me the envelope.

The envelope was empty. I looked at my medical colleague and shrugged my shoulders with my hands out, palms up, as if to say, "What is this?"

He yelled, "I'll explain later."

When we got back to shore he explained that the whole episode was a drill to see if the doctors could respond to a medical emergency.

I wasn't happy. "You mean I left my busy clinic with real sick patients to race out to a ship to pick up an empty envelope as part of a drill?" I said. Amazed, I went back to the clinic and took care of the patients who needed care and couldn't reschedule.

I continued to work hard to care for the families who came to see me. I developed a good rapport with most families and a good reputation as a caring doctor.

At one point I received a review. It was a personal evaluation for my record from the captain at the naval hospital in Naples. I had never met him and he had never been to our humble place of work. The captain wrote the review without a visit. It was a standard, generically worded review that didn't reflect any of my true experience at the island clinic.

As luck would have it the captain was scheduled to visit the clinic shortly after I received his review. I decided to talk to him about it when he came, despite my CPO's advice to let it drop. I wanted my review to reflect more of the truth.

The captain was a large, round man. He came into the clinic, made quick greetings, and whizzed his way to our third-floor kitchen. He plopped himself in a chair next to the coffee pot and cozied up with the donuts we had bought. At a mid-morning break between patients, I was scheduled for a fifteen-minute meeting with him.

"Captain," I said after some opening chitchat. "With all due respect, I would like to talk about my review."

My review said that I had "fulfilled all my Navy obligations" and "stood and passed all inspections," and that "He and his lady attend all Navy functions." I told him about my work and said I felt I had done more than fulfill my obligations. In fact, I took on extra work by being the only full-time doctor in the clinic for a year. Heck, we never even had any inspections, I said, and my wife has nothing to do with my review.

He quickly dismissed my complaints, saying I would have to take it up with the review board and send it up the chain of command. I said goodbye soon after — I had work to do. I didn't point out the crumbs on his lips and chin. He left for Naples the same day. He didn't even stay overnight.

Months later he was relieved of his command at the naval hospital. It may have been scheduled, but I heard it was not. The naval hospital in Naples was in such disrepair that a patient was apparently caught in an elevator for hours. That led to the captain's early dismissal.

Even my trip home from La Maddalena was a memorable experience. After the ferry took us from La Mad to the main island of Sardinia, a private taxi took us from Palau to Olbia and our flight back to the mainland. The taxi driver spoke some English. He played us a tape of his own songs. His real dream was to be like Frank Sinatra. He sang cabaret-style American songs in a strong Italian accent. When we got out of his taxi he gave us the tape. "Maybe you have friends in Las Vegas or Hollywood?" he said. He thought that as Americans we might have some connections to help boost his career. I wonder: did our cabaret-singing, taxi-driving friend ever make it off the island?

We had great experiences in La Mad and in Italy. A highlight was the lovely Italian couple we got to know over many enjoyable dinners together. We even attended their wedding. When we weren't visiting with our Italian friends, we traveled throughout Italy and elsewhere in Europe. This helped us keep our sanity. But we realized it was time to return to healthier relationships within our own culture. We had very good friends, close friends, back in Washington. Sure, I had a bland review from an ousted captain, but I had learned greatly from my experiences.

Interestingly, of the four doctors who came to La Maddalena when I did, one left in a straitjacket and two left with ongoing investigations about their practice on the ship. I was the only one leaving the island with my sanity intact and no investigations. I felt a sense of accomplishment, but it was only by the grace of God that at my level of training in this isolated environment no malpractice was committed on my watch.

Arrivederci, La Maddalena.

18

THE MYSTERY OF
A MOTHER'S LOVE

After two years in Italy, I went straight back to work at Bethesda Naval Hospital, where I had done my internship right after medical school. Being back in a residency program was a relief. Yes, I was on call every fourth night at the hospital, but the grind wasn't as bad as my internship had been. It was still grueling by most people's standards, but at least as residents we had interns working for us. They were the ones who had to stay up all night, which gave us residents some respite. There were still many nights of sleep deprivation, mind you, but it was a familiar world, with fewer surprises than La Maddalena and less strenuous.

During residency I also had more flexible rotations. There were more breaks from the pediatric ward and neonatal nursery, two of the most demanding areas of work. The residents were able to take electives three months out of the year. That meant we could spend time at other hospitals and even be off the call schedule. We could actually take a month and spend it learning aspects of a subspecialty. I spent months studying pediatric cardiology, gastroenterology, and other subspecialties in pediatrics.

For the most part I spent my residency at the Naval Hospital in Bethesda going to morning reports, defending my medical decisions, and playing one-upmanship with the other residents and staff by showing off articles from the most recent pediatric journals. Being at the hospital for two years, we residents developed our own clientele whom we followed in our clinics once a week. The clinic didn't truly reflect what we would be doing in our later lives as pediatricians. It was a hospital-based clinic where the patients tended to be sicker. We spent less time caring for well children than we would do once practicing. Nonetheless, it allowed us to develop close relationships with particular families.

One family I got to know in the clinic was typical for a hospital-based pediatric setting, but they stand out in my memory as an unusual and powerful example of interpersonal relationships. I am sure many pediatricians have dealt with patients who are severely disabled. I think what is most unusual in these families is the strength of the bonds between parents and their disabled child.

My patient, Neal, was a spastic quadriplegic teenager who was incapable of verbal communication. Spastic quadriplegia is a form of cerebral palsy where a patient has no control or coordination over the muscles in his four limbs. Neal could look, smile, laugh, cry, and moan. Otherwise, he lay in his place and needed to be fed, changed, bathed, and put to bed. Neal developed severe cerebral palsy at birth from unknown causes, and for thirteen years his mother had cared for him like a baby. She only knew him as a "baby" with a stagnant neurological disease. Still their relationship was special. It was all-encompassing for his mother. She did nothing else but care for Neal. It was a full-time job. I never fully understood their relationship until he died.

I followed Neal after his admission to the hospital during my first year of residency. I saw him monthly in my clinic because of his numerous health issues. Early in my second year of residency he developed pneumonia, which was probably due to his swallowing and vomiting problems. Aspiration pneumonia is common in kids with neurological defects. At our hospital, our patients went to the adult intensive care unit because there was no separate ICU for kids. To treat his pneumonia, Neal needed to be in the ICU, but the ICU was not used to dealing with kids, and certainly not disabled kids. The nurses and adult medicine physicians were visibly nervous around Neal.

Despite their nervousness, they held their noses in the air when advice was offered about caring for Neal. He needed to be put on a ventilator and the ICU staff certainly had the expertise in respirator management. It was painful to watch their uneasy body language as they treated Neal while observing the medical arrogance when talking about his care. I don't think any of them recognized this dichotomy.

Neal never recovered. His pneumonia got worse, and he became respirator-dependent. Then he was overwhelmed with infection and sepsis and pummeled with "therapies" — some of which were hardly therapeutic or healthy at all. At the height of his treatment he had tubes giving fluid or taking fluid from every orifice in his tiny body. He was being kept alive by machines. Together with the ICU staff I spoke to the mother about the options: keep him alive on machines, or let his heart stop by withdrawing the machines.

At this point his brain was already gone, not from his inborn neurological deficits but from the pressure that the infections placed on it. Any innate brain capacity he once had was gone. After difficult hours and discussions we decided together with his mother to let him go.

The ICU staff was sympathetic, but they lacked understanding. So did I.

"This will be a relief for the mother," someone said. "She's had to shoulder all the burden," someone else added. "Now she can get on with her life," they all agreed.

We unplugged the machines, and Neal went downhill fast after being taken off the respirator. I was with his mother, who sat next to Neal crying and holding his hand as he took his last few breaths. An ICU nurse came in and out of Neal's room and out of the blue I blurted to his mother, "Would you like to hold him?"

She was taken aback, but with wide eyes she asked, "Could I?"

I asked the nurse to help me move Neal to his

mom's arms. She resisted at first. "This is very unusual, Doctor," she whispered.

"Help me or get out of my way," I shot back.

The nurse made uneasy attempts at helping and then left after we had Neal situated across his mother's lap, head in the crook of her arm for the last time. She was sobbing but stroking his face. The nurse came back with the ICU attending physician, who quickly assessed the scene and said "It's all right," to the nurse outside the door.

Neal died in his mother's arms. For this she was very grateful. I was lucky to have had the idea.

Months later she called to ask if we could meet. We met after work one day. We sat in a room and talked about his death. She was trying to process all that had happened and some of the decisions we had made. She missed him so much, and she was still hurting and suffering from her loss.

It was then I recognized the incredible love she had felt for her son. There was no "relief" of any "burden." There was no other life for her to "get on with." At the time of Neal's death, I halfheartedly agreed with the comments the ICU staff made. But what we didn't understand then was that to Neal's mom there wasn't one day of "burden." There was no "relief." This was her baby. She had lost her thirteen-year-old baby, and few people could really understand what that was like. Considering all the love she had invested, Neal's life could not be dismissed with such cold, unfeeling comments.

It took me a while to pick up on this, but I'm glad

I did. I'm also glad that I witnessed such a devoted love as theirs. In future years I would see it again, but had it not been for Neal and his mom, it would not have been as easy to understand.

19

MY LAST MILITARY ASSIGNMENT

I didn't consider my medical training over until I left the military. I had finished my formal training at Bethesda Naval Hospital but had two years left on my Navy contract. Luckily, I wasn't sent overseas again, but that didn't make my experience any less interesting than my work abroad.

I was sent to Great Lakes Naval Medical Center, a military hospital in Illinois. At that time, Navy medicine was in shambles. Doctors were leaving the Navy as quickly as they could. Navy hospitals were being run with a mixture of military doctors, Veterans Administration doctors, and doctors contracted from civilian hospitals. Some services couldn't be provided by the patchwork of doctors at the Navy hospitals, so Navy patients had to be referred to civilian hospitals for specialty care. All this added up to a system that was costing the government a lot, yet breaking down at all levels.

Nowhere was this more apparent than at Great Lakes Naval Medical Center. The doctors there were caring for a high-volume, high-demand clientele. The volume was high because a boot camp was nearby, and the hospital was responsible for treating the many recruits and their young families. The patients' demands were high because many Navy personnel view their health care as free, and came to the hospital more frequently and for less serious ailments than civilians would typically do. This was in the middle of a crippling staff shortage caused by several factors, including the Navy's inability to retain doctors at higher ranks. Many Navy doctors were lured to civilian practice by higher salaries and greater freedom in administration.

The lack of older, more experienced doctors in the hospital's administration meant it wasn't clear who was running the place. The lack of older Navy doctors also meant the young Navy doctors were frequently chosen to serve on the hospital's administrative committees. At one point I was on four committees, even though I was only thirty at the time and hadn't had any administrative experience. The committees tried to address a range of quality-of-care issues that the hospital was mandated to oversee, but the committees' work was largely ineffective because the hospital was so understaffed.

The hospital was continually pressured to improve its staffing. But in order to be on staff, a physician needed to be approved by the Credentials Committee after a three-month period of temporary credentials. I sat on the Credentials Committee when one particular obstetrician applied for permanent credentials. I spoke out against his application because of the history of babies suffering severe complications from his performing Caesarean sections. The decision was put on hold. Between meetings, I was sent a letter excluding me from the committee. At the next meeting, the doctor received his full privileges. Desperate for staff, the hospital administration pushed the committee to overlook quality in its decisions to hire permanent staff.

During another committee assignment, I was asked to look into long wait times at one of the hospital's outpatient clinics. People there had to wait four hours or more and then often ended up seeing a doctor other than the one with whom they had made the appointment. I spoke to the head of the department, a civilian physician. He and his civilian colleagues were contracted by the Navy hospital, but they held positions at other facilities as well. He told me that in their contract with the Navy hospital, they were required to be accessible so patients could easily make appointments. So the doctors allowed appointments to be freely made, even though they often had no intention of being at the Navy hospital on those days due to their other commitments. In theory, their appointments would be covered by the doctors who were there. In theory. The result was a terribly overbooked clinic.

I tried to make the department chief understand that the spirit of their contract was for his staff to provide access to real appointments, not fictitious ones. He never changed his policy. When I went to the captain of the hospital about the issue, he said he couldn't force the civilian doctor to do anything because as a civilian he was not under the captain's command.

These were just two of many examples I could cite. I had seen enough to conclude that the erosion of service to military patients had gone far enough. I wrote to National Public Radio about the issue, and NPR took my story and did a three-part series on the "medical meltdown" in the military. NPR verified with other physicians what I had seen: an exodus of doctors to civilian practice, subcontracting of medical services to civilian groups because of inadequate military medical staffing, increasing referral of patients to outside civilian hospitals, rising costs, and worsening service.

I felt I had done a service to the American people and servicemen by making them aware of the obstacles facing military medicine. For me, it was time to move on. I was looking forward to practicing in a good practice with bright colleagues. I wanted to gain experience and become a well-rounded pediatrician in a warm and welcoming community. I was hoping I could practice without the distractions I had in the military. The Navy had paid for my education, but through all I experienced while working for them, I felt I had adequately paid them back.

While in the Navy, I heard from friends who left the Navy before me. They told me what I would find in a civilian practice: more competent colleagues, better salaries, more organization, and a lot less stressful work environment. Little did I know that the civilian system wouldn't stay unbroken for long.

PART II

A BROKEN
HEALTH CARE SYSTEM

20

OUR SYSTEM IS BROKEN

After practicing medicine in the civilian sector for more than twenty years, I can say without any doubt that our system is broken. Doctors are leaving for jobs outside of clinical practice. The number of uninsured is rising. Hospitals are closing. Emergency rooms are over-crowded. Doctors are being laid off. Doctors are refusing to serve patients who have certain insurances. Doctors are being pushed to see more and more patients just to maintain their salaries. Some people are seeking alternatives to traditional medicine. The quality of care is down, and the connections that we make with patients — the connections that make it all worthwhile — are weakening.

Comparisons with the rest of the world show how badly our medical system is doing. The World Health Organization, at the time of this writing, ranked the

United States thirty-seventh in the world in the delivery of health care services to its people despite the fact we spend more per person on health care than any other country. It is shocking to repeat that number — thirty-seventh in the world. In this country only ten percent of people get the best medicine money can buy, but the rest do not. We have the money and the capability to do better.

We must hope changes will be made to stem the flood in our health care system, but before things improve, we have to take a hard look at how badly broken our system truly is. More people need to understand what it takes to practice medicine in this country and which aspects of our medical system need to be strengthened to more effectively deliver health care to those who need it.

21

THE PUSH FOR THE MAX

Our health care system is full of inefficiencies. Certainly there are problems associated with expensive testing, rising pharmaceutical costs, and rising insurance premiums. One small part of our inefficient health care system is our societal push for the maximum. There are times when we must "push for the max" in order to save a life, but there are many times when the push for the max is inappropriate.

Years ago I read about baseball legend Mickey Mantle and his failing health. Having grown up in New York, I was saddened to see the great Mick in decline. Even though I detested his Yankees — remember, I was a Mets fan — I felt for him as he neared the end. For me, Mantle's demise forced me to think about my own age. If this baseball great of my youth was dying, then I, too, must be getting old.

It was 1995. I watched daily as news reports spoke of The Mick's failing liver. Eventually it became apparent that the only way he could be saved was through a liver transplant. Though he was not on the list for very long, he received a liver transplant in a short time. I suppose others didn't want the Yankee great to die either.

A short time after his liver transplant, The Mick died anyway. Because he was famous he received everything modern medicine had to offer. I don't know if I was the only one to wonder whether it was a wise use of resources. Could someone else have received that liver and lived longer with it? Was Mickey Mantle really a good transplant candidate, or did his status as a baseball legend move him up the list?

I have seen similar high-profile cases where transplants were given to well-to-do or prominent people, only for them to die anyway. I have also seen data about different groups of people who get fewer transplants than other groups, particularly black Americans. I must conclude that our medical resources are not given out justly or economically to the appropriate patients.

I remember the case of a nine-year-old boy who by all accounts had a terminal case of leukemia. Several "second" opinions confirmed this conclusion. The child's insurance wouldn't pay for the child's only hope — an experimental bone marrow transplant.

The father appealed to his community, and the furor over the insurance company's refusal to pay for the procedure led to a fund-raising campaign. The campaign succeeded in raising the needed money, and the boy finally received his bone marrow transplant. Within months the child died anyway. After the boy died, the father committed suicide.

This story is very tragic. But the blame must be placed on society's push for the maximum. We won't accept the idea that there is a time to stop doing and a time to just allow what is to be.

People who disagree say there is always hope, and there is never a time to stop trying to keep people alive. True, there are always the miracle cases, but as someone who believes and has seen some of these miracles, I know that they are rare. I am not sure we should spend enormous amounts of money trying for miracles. This is especially true where in some parts of our own society we have infant mortality rates equal to those of Third World countries, and we have millions unable to get simple antibiotics for treatable infections.

Maybe the health maintenance organization (HMO) system was too restrictive for Americans. Under the HMO system, everyone who belonged to an HMO paid one price that covered their health care needs. But what happened in this country was in an effort to contain costs, HMOs put limits on what they would pay for their members' treatments, medicines, emergency room visits. Many people complained about those restrictions, saying they had a right to top-of-the-line care and that the HMOs shouldn't limit what they would pay for treatments and medicines. In response, the HMOs agreed to pay for many of these top-of-the-line treatments and medicines, but now health insurance premiums are rising sharply every year.

As we see these increases in insurance premiums, how do we create a balance between the premiums paid to the insurance companies and the medical expenditures they incur? As we consider that important question, we as Americans must consider changing our health care expectations. We must think about how to keep from always "pushing for the max."

22

GOOD SAMARITANS

A friend from medical school and I once shared similar experiences. He told me a story about a time he and his wife went to dinner. It was a special occasion, so they went to a nice restaurant. They were sipping wine when a woman stood up with her hands to her neck and distress on her face. While other patrons began to panic, my friend reacted immediately. He grabbed the woman from behind and performed a perfect Heimlich maneuver. Up came the piece of food and the woman caught her breath. She thanked him, and they went back to their dinners.

He had saved her life.

The restaurant maître d' and the waiters were very pleased that the woman did not die in their restaurant. To show their appreciation the restaurant gave my friend and his wife every delicacy the chef could muster.

At the end of the evening they received no check. It was all on the house.

Not long after that experience, I was out to dinner at a family restaurant with my wife and some friends. Before we started our meal, a woman across the restaurant stood up from her chair. She put her hands to her neck and she, too, had a look of distress on her face. I noticed her because she was in my line of sight over my wife's shoulder.

I stood and ran over. Few people noticed what was happening. She was a big woman, and my arms barely fit around her. I quickly administered the Heimlich maneuver and fortunately my grip was just strong enough for it to work. The food came out, and I got her to her seat just before she fainted. She came around quickly, and was breathing easily within a few moments. She thanked me, and we went back to our meals.

Back at our table, my wife and friends were amazed at my quick action. The restaurant's waiters, on the other hand, seemed embarrassed by the whole situation. For the rest of my meal it seemed that my presence brought up bad memories for the staff. They couldn't wait for me to leave. No free wine. No free meal. Just scowls aimed at our table. The lesson for me was, if you want a free meal for saving someone with the Heimlich maneuver, only do it in the fanciest restaurants.

My friend and I still laugh about the story. But the episodes raised serious issues. In these emergencies, while both of us acted without hesitation, and we both did the right thing, the law gives us that freedom to act in an emergency. The Good Samaritan law allows doctors to act in a public emergency without risk of being sued. So, if while doing the Heimlich maneuver I had fractured the woman's ribs, I could not have been sued. I was able to practice urgent medicine without the fear of lawsuit.

That's not the case when it comes to non-emergency medicine these days. From our first day of training and for the rest of our careers, we doctors practice C.Y.A. (Cover Your Ass) medicine. Physicians order additional tests every day, not because they are really needed, but because they want to cover themselves in case of a lawsuit. This leads to large medical expenses. It is the largest behind-the-scenes cause of high-cost medicine in the U.S.

The threat of lawsuits — not the desire to give quality health care — guides the practice of medicine across this country. I can't help but wonder how many Good Samaritans are practicing medicine. Is there a way to protect them from lawsuits? Could there be a "Good Samaritan in Practice" law, so conscientious physicians with high satisfaction scores, great availability, and close follow-up with their patients could have less liability in lawsuits? This could motivate physicians to have strong bonds with their patients again, and return to the traditionally close doctor—patient relationship. I know, I know. This is only a pipedream. But we have to dream.

23

MEDICINE BY THE NUMBERS

When I left the Navy in 1989, I looked for a workplace where I could be comfortable. I remember interviewing for one practice that had a large number of patients with Medicaid, the federal health insurance for low-income families and the disabled. The doctors worked long hours each day, and the payments they received from Medicaid were lower than what insurance companies would pay. In order for those doctors to make decent salaries by pediatricians' standards, they had to see more patients and work longer hours. Their clientele was racially and economically diverse, which interested me. But their work hours were long.

Another practice I interviewed with was in a well-to-do town. They practiced in an area of well-insured people, and they worked at a more leisurely pace and made more money than the first practice. The reimbursements they received from the insurance companies were much higher than Medicaid, and allowed them to see fewer patients and still make good money. The majority of their patient population was white, and those patients often dictated their care because the doctors didn't want to displease their high-paying customers.

My third option was a staff model HMO. A staff-model HMO is one in which doctors are paid salaries to work exclusively for that health maintenance organization. The HMO accepted Medicaid patients through a deal with the state. Their client base was mixed, and most received health insurance paid for by their employers. I would be paid a salary, so I didn't have to worry about racing through patients to earn a decent income. The pace was dictated by how well the HMO was doing.

I chose the third option. The other options seemed like such businesses. The number of patients seen per day and reimbursements from insurers were driving forces behind the practices. Coming out of the Navy, I wanted no part of that business life. A salaried position at a staff model HMO was fine for me.

Ten years later, with HMOs teetering on the brink due to their inability to keep costs down, it was time for me to leave the HMO I had been working for and search for a new practice life. Once again I interviewed in different settings, and once again I discovered that productivity — the number of patients a doctor sees — and reimbursements were important details. By this time it didn't matter if the population was covered by Medicaid or private insurance. All practices were struggling, no matter if they were in high- or low-income areas. Nobody could join a practice anymore because practices weren't growing and didn't need doctors. Instead, you had to be taking some other doctor's place because practices did not want to risk having a decline in productivity per doctor.

What had changed in ten years was that reimbursements from Medicaid and private insurers had dropped substantially. This meant all doctors, not just pediatricians, had to work harder and see more patients to maintain the same salaries. *Medical Economics* magazine published reports in the late nineties about the stagnant salaries of internal medicine doctors and pediatricians. In this environment, many practices stopped growing. Few were hiring. Some weren't hiring even as they lost physicians to retirement. The result was a very tight job market for pediatricians. Fortunately, I found a small practice where a pediatrician had retired, and the practice was busy enough to need me.

This experience of looking for a job in two different eras — first at the height of HMO growth in the 1980s and then during the HMO downfall a decade later — demonstrated a dramatic change in medicine. Practitioners could no longer practice without an eye toward the business aspect. As costs rose, doctors were placed between insurers and patients. Often their salaries hinged on how many patients they saw and how conservative their spending was. There was nowhere to hide. By the end of the nineties, few doctors were being paid a salary. Almost all doctors' annual incomes were based in part on incentives to see more and more patients. We were no longer caring for patients. We were counting the numbers.

24

SEVENTY PATIENTS A DAY

An experience I once had illustrates the dangers of high patient productivity in pediatrics. I was in transition, looking for a practice outside my failing HMO. I found a temporary position in a practice where an older pediatrician was retiring. At first it seemed to be a good fit, though the older doctor, Dr. Bjorn, didn't give me an exact time when he planned to retire. "Maybe six months. Maybe a year." he said.

When I got the chance to witness his practice, it convinced me that the kids would benefit from his retirement. Dr. Bjorn's practice was appallingly bad. He took pride in seeing sixty to seventy patients a day, yet he would be done by 4:30 in the afternoon. That obviously meant he wasn't spending time listening to parents and their issues. This was reflected in the way some of his patients' concerns were handled.

Dr. Bjorn saw patients for minutes at a time. He treated everyone (and I mean everyone) with antibiotics. Unfortunately, a lot of his patients came to believe antibiotics were the answer to everything.

The problem with this approach is obvious and well-publicized. Today, experts have recommended widespread curbs on antibiotic use. Resistant strains of bacteria are becoming problematic because antibiotics are being overused. In truth, only a small percentage of infections actually need antibiotics.

The other problem with the indiscriminate use of antibiotics is that many patients are treated the wrong way for their problem. Children with asthma are put on antibiotics and not on the asthma medicines that they critically need. Some go months using antibiotics while suffering with their asthma symptoms. The asthma medicines take more time in the office because teaching patients how to use them is so important in their use. Perhaps that was one reason Dr. Bjorn didn't use them.

Dr. Bjorn's motivation, however, was never in doubt. He often told me how his stocks were doing, and he repeatedly spoke about the money he was drawing from the practice. He openly bragged to me about the number of patients he saw per day, as if he were shooting for a new record. All the while he thought, "Practice is easy."

If patients stayed in his practice long enough, they discovered that some things were being missed. I saw one child whom Dr. Bjorn had sent to an orthopedic surgeon. To begin with, the father didn't understand why his son was sent to orthopedics. He told me that he had complained to the doctor that his boy was squirming in his pants too much. Before inquiring much, Dr. Bjorn sent him to the orthopedic surgeon.

When I visited with the boy, I did some questioning and a simple test to check for parasites in his anal area. I diagnosed the boy with a parasitic infection of his bowel. The parasite was the pinworm, a common condition that gives kids a seriously itchy butt. The boy didn't need an orthopedic surgeon, just some time, patience, and a simple test.

I saw another child who was in for an annual physical. The year before, he had been seen by Dr. Bjorn, and the mother had told the doctor about a lump in her son's groin. Dr. Bjorn told her not to worry about it.

The mother showed me the lump. It was an obvious large hernia. The boy had spent a year with a dangerously enlarged hernia. He had it repaired within a week of his visit with me, but I was shocked that such an easy diagnosis could be missed. The only explanation was that Dr. Bjorn must have done only a cursory exam on the boy.

Another family came to me and would not tell me much about their six-week-old baby. They were Hispanic, but spoke English well. They wanted me to listen to their son's heart. When I listened I found that the child had a very loud heart murmur indicating a congenital defect. I asked them who their cardiologist was, since I thought they must have one already if their baby's heart murmur was that noticeable. They said they didn't have a cardiologist.

"Did you know about the murmur?" I asked.

"Yes, but Dr. Bjorn said we should just 'watch it,'" they said.

Then they revealed how they had learned about their son's problem. While visiting a friend in Florida, they had taken their son to the friend's pediatrician. The pediatrician said the baby needed to see a cardiologist right away. They drove back home immediately because they wanted to get my opinion quickly, and get their son to a cardiologist near their home in Boston.

"If this child has not been seen by a cardiologist, we need to arrange a visit to one immediately," I said. The child was seen by a pediatric cardiologist the following morning. He had a congenital heart defect and should never have gone six weeks without an evaluation.

These are just a few stories of inappropriate care by Dr. Bjorn. This wasn't about him getting older as he neared retirement and losing his skills — this was about his attitude. There are more stories. For example, his overuse of antibiotics and overdiagnosis of ear infections and tonsillitis led to a huge number of inappropriate surgeries for ear tubes and tonsillectomies. In another case, a child with a kidney disease went untreated for a time because simple tests weren't ordered.

Dr. Bjorn needed to get out before he hurt someone badly, but he decided not to. That meant there was no room for me in the practice. Fortunately, a few months later I found another practice where a doctor had already retired. It was a blessing in two ways. I got into a better practice environment and I didn't have to work with Dr. Bjorn. I had picked up his pieces for four months and that was long enough.

The scariest thing about this story is that it's not unique. Some physicians are driven by the profit motive so much that they practice "factory medicine." They want to move people through to make the most money they can. Dr. Bjorn is not the only one who practices this way. Unfortunately, with reimbursements stagnant or decreasing, many doctors have to push up productivity and see more patients to maintain their salaries. As the medical crisis in this country deepens, we must remain conscious of how insurers are pushing physicians to higher and higher productivity numbers. This could have (and has already had) catastrophic effects on the quality of care delivered to unsuspecting patients, as these stories demonstrate.

As for Dr. Bjorn, I hope he retires soon. Maybe he has by now. But until he does retire, his patients will continue to breeze through his office, overtreated for simple issues and unheard and overlooked on the complex ones.

25

THE CASE FOR
IMMUNIZATION

Why is it that pediatricians are facing more and more people who question the value of immunizing their children? This is amazing to me, since reputable organizations like the United Nations, the World Health Organization, the American Academy of Pediatrics, and the Centers for Disease Control wholeheartedly support immunizations.

It's an interesting cultural phenomenon. We live in an age when we question our government, and we have lost faith in institutions. We are losing our connection between doctors and patients and our faith in medicine. So, people question immunizations.

The evidence in favor of immunizing children is strong. The profound impact of one vaccine introduced during my career highlights what I'm talking about. When I was in training, I saw children with meningitis, epiglottis, and periorbital cellulitis — all serious bacterial illnesses caused by hemophilus influenza, or "H flu." Those illnesses hardly exist anymore in the U.S. since the introduction nearly twenty years ago of the HIb vaccine, which helps people fight illnesses caused by hemophilus influenza type-B.

There was a polio epidemic in 1956, the year I was born. Thanks to polio vaccines we now live in a time when polio may be eliminated worldwide. Sure, the smallpox vaccine left a scar on the shoulder of anyone thirty-five and older in this country. But since smallpox has been eliminated, nobody needs that vaccine anymore. It's clear to me that immunizations benefit individuals as well as society as a whole. Vaccines are safer now than they've ever been, yet people suspect the opposite.

There is now closer scrutiny of vaccines than ever before. Since 1999, some vaccines have been pulled from the market because of suspicions about their side effects, while the composition of other vaccines has been changed to decrease the risk of side effects.

Many questions people have about vaccines are based only on timing. People assume the immunization caused the problem only because the problem appeared close to or just after the vaccine was given. But timing does not prove cause and effect. Nevertheless, the Internet is loaded with poor information and stories that terrify people about vaccines. It's a shame that people don't look at reputable organizations and their Web sites before they refuse vaccines for their children. The Centers for Disease Control, the World Health Organization, and the American Academy of Pediatrics all provide good information parents can rely on.

Deciding against vaccines is like buying an old car that hasn't been safety-tested and deciding that the car must be safe and reliable because it has been around forever. From a safety standpoint, it would make more sense to buy a newer car that has been safety-tested and has a great safety record. The same goes for immunizations.

There is an inherent risk in buying and using a car, whether it's old or new. At least the new safety-tested car reduces your risk. The old way of going through childhood results in many deaths and illnesses. The new childhood — with vaccines — is safer.

Immunizations are an issue of trust. Trust between patients and doctors. Trust between people and the U.S. health care system. In August 2001, *Consumer Reports* magazine published an article about vaccine safety entitled, "Vaccines: an Issue of Trust." People trust vaccines less because they trust the health care system less.

Is it any wonder that people who are getting disenfranchised by the medical industry are having trouble trusting the system? No.

Is this issue of trust a growing problem for American medicine that needs to be addressed? Yes.

26

THE MOVE TOWARD ALTERNATIVE MEDICINE

"Alternative" is a word suggesting one has options. It implies there is a path you can choose other than the one most commonly taken. "Alternative medicine" today refers to the options people are choosing over "traditional medicine." It's interesting that people are choosing these alternatives, but what's even more interesting is that traditional medicine is beginning to recognize it.

Today doctors can attend conferences to learn about herbal medicine, homeopathic medicine, chiropractic medicine, and acupuncture. There is a movement to have these forms of medicine accepted by practitioners of traditional medicine. In fact, some insurance companies are covering the costs of these alternative medicines. In Canada, these alternatives are also covered.

When I started practicing twenty years ago I encountered few people who were using alternative forms of medicine. Now I practice in the same building as an acupuncturist, and every day patients ask me about alternatives to the medicine I offer. I have had to gain a perspective on alternative medicine, and find out where I stand on it.

There are forms of alternative medicine I have learned to believe in and rely on. For example, I often refer people to massage therapy for muscle aches and pains, and my wife and I have used acupuncture with some success. Frankly, I believe medicine benefits by having more of these options available to patients. The reality is that in traditional medicine, we tend to rely heavily on medicines, whereas alternative practices sometimes offer treatments just as effective for certain illnesses and less invasive to the body.

However, another aspect of the growth of alternative medicine bothers me. Why are people turning away from traditional medicine? I fear it is because of a failure within our system. Do people find alternative medicine more personal? More available? Easier to access? Does the field of alternative medicine provide patients with a greater sense of control? I believe all these are true.

Traditional medicine has become such a complex business that it's difficult even for doctors to understand it all. I believe the growth in alternative medicine is another sign of people losing trust in our health care system. I don't blame the patients or the practitioners of alternative medicine. The blame lies within our system of medicine. Many things need to be fixed. We need to regain the trust of patients, improve our availability, and become more personal. People need to feel cared for. They need to feel their health is being taken care of in a personal way. But unless our bureaucratic world of medicine changes its ways and starts giving people those feelings, people are going to explore alternatives.

27

MEDICINE AS SEEN ON TV

Pharmaceutical companies send representatives to doctors' offices every day. It happens behind the scenes, and few patients are aware of the encounters, but here's how it works: Each drug company sends representatives, and they provide us with samples of their drugs for us to give away.

They also provide lunches, dinners, snacks, and gifts for the office. Every month, our office receives pens, cups, paperweights — all prominently labeled with the names of the companies' drugs. Every other month, the drug companies send us free lunches — pizza, pasta meals, gourmet sandwiches. Practically every week they offer conferences for our "continued medical education." These conferences are often held over lunch or dinner and include a free meal for the doctors who attend.

It wasn't always like this. Years ago, drug companies demonstrated to doctors why their drug worked better than others. Today, pharmaceutial companies have a different emphasis. They provide conferences that are often biased in favor of the company's medicines. Speakers at the conference or the company's representatives recommend the new drugs to the doctors in attendance as the best way to treat specific illnesses. Couple this type of marketing with all the advertising on television and you have a system where the company with the best marketing makes the most off its medicines.

Patients will come in asking for certain medicines they have seen advertised on television, and doctors are pressured to use certain drugs because of the "bribes" they have received from drug companies. What you end up with is high-cost pharmaceuticals being prescribed instead of low-cost alternatives. Many times the "greater efficacy" claimed by higher-cost medicines is questionable, but of course that is lost in all the marketing efforts. Today, pharmaceutical companies spend proportionally more on marketing and less on new product development.

Let me give an example. Many years ago there were few medicines available to treat Attention Deficit Hyperactivity Disorder (ADHD). Because of the increasing number of ADHD cases diagnosed, those few existing reliable medicines made a good amount of money. Soon other drug companies jumped on the bandwagon. Recognizing an area where profits could be made, several companies made variations of the existing ADHD medicines and marketed them as the "newest" and "longest lasting" on the market. Now, pediatricians are pressured by companies and parents to use these new variations first. In the end, it's the same old medicines being used in new forms at twice the cost.

The pharmaceutical industry has enjoyed a boom over the last ten to twenty years. If the current system is allowed to continue, drug costs will continue to rise and the medical industry may go bust. There is a way to insure that people who need medicines get them at a reasonable price, but for that to happen we have to turn back the clock. Years ago pharmaceutical companies only marketed through doctors' groups. Direct advertising to consumers through television commercials or magazine ads did not exist in the field. That meant companies had to convince an association of well-informed doctors that their medicines truly worked and were the best option. That way, the most effective medicines were prescribed instead of just the best-marketed ones.

In this time of high costs, shouldn't we return to a system like that? But the profits that pharmaceutical companies earn are a strong incentive not to change the current, corrupt system. Consumers will continue to be convinced that the expensive medicine they saw last night on television is just the one they need. And despite the cost to insurers, they are likely to get it prescribed. Ultimately, insurers pay more for the high-cost, well-marketed medicines, and consumers end up seeing their health insurance premiums skyrocket, which leads more and more people to being unable to afford any health insurance at all.

28

SUED

I have approached my practice life as a Good Samaritan. I have a long history of service to my patients and my community. I have received awards that demonstrate my commitment to service. It was this passionate commitment to service that made it so hurtful to be sued. How could someone sue me when I am so dedicated to my work for them?

At first I didn't believe that I was the one being sued. With all the mail I receive, much of it from lawyers making inquiries, I hardly batted an eye when I saw my name on top of a notification from the lawyers. After all, in the past I had been asked to testify in numerous court cases. It took two or three attempts from my lawyer to reach me, and even after we spoke I could not believe this time I was the one being sued.

My lawyer tried to impress upon me that this was

a real case and it would be a bitter fight. I was sued for examining and discharging a normal newborn baby who two weeks later had a seizure and years later was diagnosed with autism. I was accused of providing poor breast-feeding counseling that supposedly led to the seizure that apparently led to the autism. I continued to dismiss it as ridiculous. I just couldn't believe I was being sued for breastfeeding counseling. I quickly realized how wrong I was when I was soundly battered in my first deposition. That's when I realized this was serious. They were indeed making a case out of what I did or didn't do. I was on the defensive.

I got more serious about my approach to the case for my second deposition and put forward a better presentation. Nevertheless, my lawyer saw that I needed more preparation, so we entered a world of the legal profession few know exist. I met with a professional witness consultant — a lawyer who specializes in coaching doctors on how to defend themselves in court. I was videotaped and coached on how to present myself to the jury. I was critiqued on facial movements, posture, tone, and demeanor. We went through a mock trial that was set up as a real case in front of a paid jury. Even expert witnesses were paid to testify.

We won the case before the mock jury. The preparation process made me more confident, since I had nearly lost faith in myself and my medical skills during the grilling of the depositions. The opposing lawyer had made me feel incompetent. The lawsuit had questioned my abilities, and now I was questioning them too. Had I really been at fault after all?

The emotional ups and downs endured for years. Postponements and reschedulings were the rule, not the exception. Finally, after almost three years from my first deposition, we went to trial.

The case took five weeks due to holidays and the availability of the judge. Their side put forward twelve expert witnesses to our five. They presented their case the first four weeks and we defended for one week. In the end the jury found me not guilty in little over a day of deliberation. After years of agonizing self-doubt and the fear of a tainted reputation for the rest of my practice life, I was finally feeling not guilty.

The jury sympathized with my plight. They were never swayed by the plaintiff's argument. I know because one juror called me after the case ended. He and I had been exchanging looks for five weeks. I thought I saw sympathy in his eyes, but I could not be certain what he saw in mine. After all, we were not allowed to speak to each other while the trial was under way. I was fortunate that this kind man called me after it was all over. We spoke on the phone for a while, and then he arranged to meet with me and some other jurors. Together we commiserated. We all had our lives stopped for five weeks. Our family lives had been torn apart. Our earnings had been cut for over a month. We were infuriated by the whole process.

It was hard for us to understand how the case got to court in the first place. The case is as farfetched on paper as in the courtroom. I was only partially responsible for breast-feeding counseling; most of it is the responsibility of nurse practitioners in obstetrics, who spend large amounts of time with the mother before she leaves the hospital. So how did this case get to court? And how did it last five weeks in court, occupying fifteen jurors, four lawyers, two doctors (I had one colleague who was a co-defendant), and a judge?

The story is one of power. The father,, also an M.D., had connections to well-known and influential pediatricians from one of the best children's hospitals in the world. He recruited these doctor friends to testify on his son's behalf. When the case was initially reviewed to determine whether it should go to trial, the judge saw the lineup of pediatric "stars" and assumed the case was court-worthy. The case lasted a long time because the plaintiff's legal team insisted on using its entire lineup of experts even though all their testimony never amounted to a coherent case. The whole spectacle demonstrated that if you have enough power and the right lawyers behind you, you can force a case, and you may just get something if the other side is willing to back down. Thankfully, my lawyers weren't intimidated.

Ironically, the case was lost on their first witness — the child's mother. In her testimony about her problems with breast-feeding, she admitted to regularly using a bottle to feed her baby. How could the family argue that poor breast-feeding caused the dehydration that led to the baby's seizure and autism when the mother was also bottle-feeding her baby? My juror friend told me he and the other jurors were convinced the first day in court that my accusers didn't have a case against me. The jurors just had to wait five weeks to give their decision.

Even though the lawsuit was so obviously frivolous, the trauma of going through it made me doubt myself, and question everything I do as a doctor. Such malpractice lawsuits are enough to crush the desire of anyone in the medical field.

With all the emphasis on malpractice in medicine, few people recognize that doctors win the great majority of malpractice lawsuits against them. Of those malpractice suits won by patients, very few get large awards like those seen in the newspapers. It is those big winners that drive the insane number of malpractice cases in our country. Malpractice experts say that every doctor graduating from medical school will be sued at least once. Having been through it myself, I do not wish that fate on any of them.

29

STREET MEDICINE

For five or six years, I volunteered on a medical van for the homeless. The van was a modified camper van with benches behind the driver's compartment that served as a waiting room. Going toward the back of the van, a hallway led from the waiting room to a sink and lab area. Then a door led to an exam room at the tail of the camper. The van was run by a nonprofit group called Bridge over Troubled Waters. It traveled nightly to four stops in Boston and Cambridge. The goal was to find homeless people on the streets and let them see a doctor or nurse practitioner. Medical personnel volunteered on the van once or twice a month. Without the van, many people on the streets would not have gotten care for even the simplest infections. And without my experience on the van, I would not have learned about the world of the inner-city homeless.

The van took me into a clandestine world not seen by many Americans. When the van made a stop, social workers would go out to canvass for clients. Many times they would find someone on the street who was sick, and bring them to the van for treatment. Though the van served homeless of all ages, the social workers targeted people from their young teens to mid-twenties. I learned a lot about the people living on the streets. In the winter, they kept warm by the heat given off by buses or the grates over subway tunnels. They squatted in vacant homes. They met in garages and parks. I read the newspaper that was written and sold by the homeless.

I learned about young runaways bumming their way across the U.S. I saw kids on the van who would say to each other, "Hey, didn't I see you in San Francisco last week?" I saw kids who were hurt and shunned by their families — often rich families. The kids couldn't live up to expectations, so they fled.

The street kids got to know where the van stopped and the times it would arrive. They often stopped in for hot chocolate in the winter or lemonade in the summer. Then I would hear their stories, or see them for their medical problems.

They came to the van with a wide variety of health problems — from ingrown toenails because of poor fitting shoes, to pneumonia from living without protection from the elements. Some kids had asthma but no medication for it. Young pregnant women were also among the van visitors, joining friends in their underground travels through Boston and other cities.

They were interesting people from various backgrounds. They all had problems but few were "crazy," as many people assume when talking about people who live on the street.

Many people living on the street end up with severe medical problems that eventually require hospitalization, but if we don't look hard enough we won't see them. And if we don't reach out, we don't have to treat them either — at least not until their problems are so severe they end up in the hospital.

This type of outreach is critical to our health care system. Every time a doctor from the van treats an asthmatic patient or someone with pneumonia, it saves our health care system thousands of dollars by preventing a more severe problem that will require hospitalization. Preventing three serious cases of asthma makes up the cost of running this kind of outreach effort for a year. This is the kind of cost-effective effort our health system needs, but there are too few of them and too few people who even know they exist.

Medical van services for the homeless have popped up in other cities as well. I no longer work on the van in Boston, but I am thankful it exists, visiting the neighborhoods of Boston and Cambridge and serving those who would otherwise not be reached.

30

INSURANCELESS

One day a five-year-old boy with asthma came in to my office. I picked up his chart and flipped through it before going into the exam room. I had seen the boy before and knew his case well. He used three medicines regularly to control his asthma. Whenever he didn't take the medicines, he often ended up in the emergency room with asthma attacks. We are fortunate to live in a time where asthma can be well-controlled with inhaled medications. In the last few years, these medicines have decreased the number of emergency room visits and hospitalizations for children with asthma. Even the death rate for kids with asthma has declined. My five-year-old patient had come to see me for a check-up and a review of his asthma status. The reviews helped us to maintain his asthma at a manageable level.

In the exam room, I greeted the boy and his mother

and reviewed his growth and physical signs. He was doing well. He had been stable on his asthma medications for several months with only one minor flare-up of asthma due to a cold. I congratulated the mother on her vigilance in caring for his asthma. She had done a great job.

Toward the end of the visit, I began to write prescriptions for refills of his asthma medicines. That's when I got hit with the bombshell. The mother asked if I could give her a few months' extra medicine because the family didn't have health insurance. "It's so expensive," she said. "My husband and I are both working but we are just able to keep our housing and car payments going. Health insurance takes such a bite. We decided to chance it for a few months. If my husband gets a second job in the spring maybe we can get insurance again."

I asked her what would happen if the boy had to go to the emergency room again. She had it all worked out. "Well, paying for even a couple of ER visits in three months is cheaper than paying for insurance for that time," she says.

I gave her three months of medicine and told her to call me when the medicine ran out, even if she didn't have insurance.

This is not an unfamiliar scenario. It's a choice that many hard-working parents are making. In the case of this five-year-old boy, both parents had jobs, and they were talking about finding a third job to be able to afford health insurance! The choice of going without health insurance can cripple a family and be devastating to a child's health. What if this boy ran out of medicine and the family still didn't have insurance? What if the boy needed more than the emergency room? What if he ended up in the intensive care unit with an asthma attack? The family could have lost their home or gone bankrupt just because they couldn't afford health insurance for a few months.

Many other families live on the periphery of our health care system. We see them as patients who claim to have insurance but don't have it. We send them bills but they never pay. Then they switch to other doctors and do the same. Or they just show up at the emergency room where they can't be turned away, and the hospital never gets paid because they're uninsured. By one account the number of people in the U.S. who go without health insurance at least part of every year is sixty-six million people, almost a quarter of the 295 million people in our country today.[1] This is the reality of our health system.

Those of us who practice medicine in this country see this in action every day. Every time I experience a case like this it irritates me that our system allows this to happen. There has to be a better way.

1. Kimball Lewis, Marilyn R. Ellwood, and John L. Czajka, "Counting the Uninsured," Urban Institute, July 1998.

31

SO ABSURD IT'S FUNNY

Patrick needed a follow-up for his strep throat. In the past several months, this seven-year-old boy had had strep several times. We tried to coax him to allow me to do the strep test by opening his mouth wide, but he didn't like being gagged by the tongue depressor. He tried to negotiate how we would do the strep test. He wanted to do it sitting up. Then the next minute he wanted to do it lying down. Ultimately, we had to lay him down and quickly force his mouth open, gag him as gently as possible, and swab his throat with a long set of Q-tips. After this rough treatment I asked him whether he was still my friend. He said he was and forgave me for the rough treatment. Now all we had to do was wait for the strep results, which would take five minutes. We chatted while we waited.

His mother told me she wouldn't be surprised if he

needed his tonsils out, because it had been that kind of year for the family. They had been through enough trauma in the past year that it was a surprise they were still functioning. The problems had begun the summer before when her husband had lost the sales job he had held for four years. He had been the sole breadwinner and when he lost his job the family lost all their benefits, including health insurance.

To hold things together until he could find another job, both of these college-graduate parents took jobs with no benefits. The mother took a job as a waitress/bartender, but on her first shift at the bar she suffered a bizarre back/spinal cord injury. At thirty-eight, she ruptured a thoracic disk, one of the spongy pads between the vertebrae. In her case, the ruptured disk was pressing against the spinal cord, causing great pain and posing a danger of neurological damage. This was an unusual injury for someone her age, and rare for a woman. She needed emergency surgery at a Boston hospital. The situation was serious. Going into the surgery, doctors told her husband that his wife might never walk again. The surgery was extremely delicate, they told him. His wife could die.

The surgery was absolutely necessary. There were no choices, no second opinions. There was also no waiting. Her surgery was done in the middle of the night and took seven hours. It was successful, but still there was no guarantee of a full recovery. In fact, her prognosis was grim. Luckily, after a few days there was reason for hope — she could move her toes. There was progress almost daily for a while. Her recovery was painful and difficult. After regaining most of the sensation and movement in her legs, the recovery slowed to a crawl. She needed many months of physical therapy to strengthen her legs, and her gait was off for the better part of a year. As a former runner, she was anxious to get back on the road, but nine months after surgery, she still fell occasionally while running.

A year after her surgery, her life was starting to get back to somewhere near normal. Her husband had found a good job with benefits. She was doing some freelance communications consulting. Their two boys had had mild health problems, particularly with repeated cases of strep. As I listened to the family trauma of the past year, her son and I played with my toys. He had his two favorites out — Buzz Lightyear and Thomas the Tank Engine. Quite a combination. As his mother finished her story, the little boy interjected that I could come over to his house and play with his toys sometime. I told him that maybe I would someday.

His strep test came back negative. That was a relief. Maybe we wouldn't have to remove his tonsils, and we could just hope he didn't get any more strep that year.

I told his mother how lucky I thought they had been. To go through unemployment, a major physical injury, children's injuries, and the depletion of some savings all in one year is a lot for any family. Certainly such a year could ruin any family, especially when one member is left with a disability. But the family hadn't been destroyed, despite all that had happened. I also felt they were lucky the medical catastrophe they had experienced hadn't completely depleted their finances, since they didn't have insurance at the time. The mother told me that she was surprised, too. At the time of their visit with me, they had not received one hospital bill, she said.

Her son was grabbing for my attention. We were trying to have him put away the toys. It was time to go, but he was reluctant to leave. He had gone from a crying boy who was forced to get a throat culture to a happy playmate. He invited me to his birthday party, and I told him I would try to come. His mother whispered that no such party was planned, and his birthday was still months away. I reassured her that I get invited to birthday parties every week but I have yet to attend one.

We coaxed him out to the front desk, and after I bribed him with a sticker, he willingly left with his mother. After they had gone I worried for the family. They really had undergone a tough year and they had made it through, but I had a feeling of dread that another shoe was going to drop.

The next morning the mother called. When she got home from our appointment she had opened an envelope from the hospital. It was a $14,000 bill for her neurosurgical team. It hadn't taken too long for that other shoe to drop.

We chatted for a while again. She told me it was just so absurd that you had to laugh. In fact, she told me that was how they had gotten through the past year. The family stayed together by enjoying laughs whenever they could, even in the face of hard times. The latest episode was no different. Paying a bill so large was impossible, so impossible it was funny that anyone would even send such a bill. Did they really think a family could pay a bill for $14,000? Few families in the United States could pay such a bill. The family would have to figure out eventually what to do with it, but for now the absurdity of receiving such a huge bill after such a long road of financial and physical recovery was just too funny to take seriously. So we laughed and hoped there was a way out.

This is the way medical care goes for millions of Americans. Those without insurance — even through no fault of their own — sometimes face financial ruin because of a catastrophic event. The mother's injury was catastrophic for this family. They now faced a life together that was different from the life they had had before, confronted with bills that could deplete their savings and change their financial future. It wasn't fair, but that's the system we have in the U.S. — a system that is markedly unfair to millions of families across the country including hard-working, educated families like this one.

32

DOCTORS REACT

We have already seen how doctors react to the pressures in medicine by cranking up their hours and numbers of patients. Their annual earnings have remained the same or fallen year after year, even though they are seeing more patients. To keep earning the same pay, they are adding to their already busy work lives. What does that do to patient service? Is this a sustainable way to do business?

Doctors are not standing still in this medical climate. Several initiatives are being taken to ward off the pressure. The most common reaction is the formation of doctors into networks. This empowers them to wield power as a group and pressure the insurance companies for higher reimbursements.

One recent summer, a group of doctors threatened not to care for patients insured by a particular company because the doctors felt the company wasn't reimbursing them enough. The doctors had cared for the patients holding that insurance for years, but had been forced more and more to subsidize parts of the patients' care because the insurance company was limiting reimbursements so much that they often didn't cover the full cost of care. It got to the point that doctors were losing money on each of the patients covered by that insurer. The doctors' group action was warranted. The insurance company took their threat seriously and increased the doctors' reimbursements. This was a landmark action by doctors. I wonder if it will lead to more group actions by doctors in the future.

Although the action by the doctors' group yielded higher reimbursements, it's not clear if it really was a "win" for doctors. The insurance company did not absorb the costs. Instead, it passed them on to consumers as higher insurance premiums and co-payments. So, for each visit to the doctor, the patient had to pay more, sometimes as much as thirty dollars per visit. At least anecdotally, I've heard that some families who can't afford the higher costs have cut their visits to the doctor as a result of the change.

Group action against insurers hasn't been doctors' only reaction. Some are bowing to the pressure from insurers by cutting back on the number of patients they see. To earn their salaries, they are charging some patients thousands of dollars on top of the insurance reimbursements. In return they promise greater access and more personalized care. This type of practice has been called "concierge medicine."

It is another form of health care directed to those who can pay. In other words: more medicine for the affluent. More services for those who can afford a higher price. It is exactly what American medicine does not need. Nevertheless, concierge medicine is growing across the country. Doesn't everyone deserve good service from their physician? Shouldn't all physicians be supportive and caring without an extra price? Shouldn't all physicians link patients to specialists when needed?

Many would argue today that the rich already get the best medicine. The last thing we need is more medicine for the people who can already afford the top insurances. It is becoming increasingly apparent that too many people are not well-served in our current medical system.

Why then, are we creating medical systems to care more for those who already have health care, while millions still lack access to basic medical services? Left to economic forces alone, it stands to reason that those who can afford less will receive worse medical service, or no medical service at all, while those who can pay will get more. We already have sectors of our society with infant mortality rates and other statistics close to those of Third World countries. We're growing closer to Third World medicine in other ways as well. In many Third World countries the wealthy receive good medical care, the poor receive health care only in emergencies, and many receive no health care at all.

Many people defend our medical system by pointing to the technology and advances written about in the newspapers. That may be true, but unfortunately our world-class medical system is administered on a very unequal basis in which people's incomes determine the care they get. As doctors react and demand more from the system and insurers demand more from patients, the gap between rich and poor in the delivery of health care continues to grow.

33

A MEDICAL EXODUS

I had three separate conversations in six months about the same subject with some of my doctor friends. They were all tired of insurance agencies, law firms, and pharmaceutical companies running their practices. They weren't enjoying themselves. All three were going to business school because they wanted to change the way their practice lives were going. They thought that if doctors were in management they could improve the world of medicine.

During the same period, I received a letter from a friend. He is a hardworking, dedicated pediatrician, but at the end of his note he asked, "Please, can you tell me when it will be fun to practice again?"

Around the same time, I saw a newspaper article about doctors changing careers. The article featured a doctor who advises other doctors about career opportunities. Her career counseling practice was booming because doctors were leaving medical practice for alternative careers in medicine, such as working in hospital administration and in pharmaceutical sales.

I was suffering from a period of disenchantment in practice. I was chief of the pediatric department for an HMO where for four or five years in a row we had been forced to cut our budget and cut services, despite having an efficient office with a highly respected staff. Somehow I internalized the problems my department was facing, and I questioned what I was doing with my life.

I went to see the career counselor. At the end of a two-hour session she said I should combine my interests in management, medicine, and public service and do "foundation" work. What she meant was I should find foundations with money and work to help them do their charitable work. For this advice I paid her a handsome fee.

Just out of curiosity, I met with a second career counselor for doctors. We met for an hour. After reviewing my résumé and credentials, she concluded that we needed to do personality and psychological evaluations. Her firm also would educate me about all the fields where doctors work. The full evaluation would take at least six weeks and cost me thousands of dollars.

Before going through with it, I decided to follow the first career counselor's advice and talk to a pediatrician friend who worked for a foundation. I felt I could pick her brain and find out if foundation work was for me.

We met at her office. After being delayed by interruptions and phone calls, she met with me for a half hour. I told her why I was there, and she asked, "You mean you think you want a job like mine?" She told me, "I know you and how you care for kids. You would miss that. And you would not like the politics, budget work, or the management work required in my job. Go back to what you do well, Brian, even if it is harder to practice these days."

My friend was right. It wasn't the caring for kids that I didn't like. I loved that part of my job. It was the practice life itself that was difficult. How many of my doctor friends had left their jobs not because their career choice was wrong but because of faults in the system? I'll never know, but I'm glad I was steered back in the right direction.

In the current practice environment doctors are struggling in their work lives. From what I see, hear, and feel doctors are highly dissatisfied with the pressures placed on them in today's medical work environment. Why is everyone so unhappy?

Since the start of the 1990s, physicians have been bearing the brunt of changes in practice life. First the HMO movement put physicians in the role of "gatekeeper." This meant that doctors were in charge of deciding whether patients would receive benefits from their insurance company. This was not a role that physicians enjoyed. Not at all. It immediately created conflict between doctors and their patients, since patients began to see doctors as the barrier to proper treatment. What a blow to what traditionally had been a trusting relationship!

During the nineties and into this decade, physicians have seen their salaries remain stagnant. In fact, in order to keep earning the same money, many doctors have had to raise their productivity by seeing more patients. And while working harder, physicians have had to pay more in premiums for malpractice insurance because there are more malpractice cases and settlements than there used to be.

The increase in malpractice cases is further evidence of the decline in trust between doctors and patients. Is it any wonder why doctors are leaving practice? What type of person would stay in a job where they are trying to do good for people but people don't trust them? It is easy for me to understand my friends' doubts about the direction of the medical profession. It is hard to be happy while working harder, not being trusted in your work, and having to answer to the whims of insurance companies.

PART III

EXPERIENCE IS A GREAT TEACHER

34

A TYPICAL VISIT

"Here he comes!"

Not a workday goes by without me hearing this phrase, only to look up and see a small boy or girl peering out from one of my exam rooms. I'd like to think they are excited to see me, their pediatrician, but perhaps it's my toys. I keep a small shaving kit full of miniature toys as part of my medical equipment. Kids look at me eagerly, hoping I offer them my shaving kit and the toys inside.

The toys are a story unto themselves. I began carrying little figurines made of plastic for the kids to play with when I worked in Italy twenty years ago. The first toys were Smurfs that I had bought in Germany. In the years since, kids have brought me toys or traded some of theirs for mine. Many of my toys have disappeared, destined for the toy box of one of my little patients if the child was able to get away without putting it back at clean-up time.

Thanks to over twenty years of formal practice, I have developed my own routine for clinic visits that makes it fun for the child and less intrusive for me. With the child enthralled by the toys spread out on the floor or in rows on the exam table, I chat with the parent and get a history. During this time I answer specific questions the parent may have. Usually it's the mother, but often the father comes too. I ask about the child's sleep and behavior, and I don't shy away from discussing those issues in depth.

I then move on to the physical examination, which the child hardly notices. While they continue to play, I listen to their heart and lungs. If a child is anxious about me looking in their ears I often have them hold up to one ear a figurine while I look "through" the other ear to see which figurine they are holding. Sometimes I listen to the heart on one of my toys before I listen to the child's heart. Other times I'll entertain them with the "boing" sound their knees make when I test their reflexes. Adding an element of play makes my exam easy and fun for kids.

Once the physical is done, we turn to the shots or blood tests. This is the dirty work of the job, but fortunately I've always had great nurses to help me. After the shots, I say goodbye. Before the tears and sobs have stopped it is common for me to hear a snuffling, "Goodbye" and "Thank you, (sniff) Doctor." It makes me sad and happy at the same time.

"See you next time," I tell them. "And you can play with my toys again — okay?" To which they slowly nod their tearful little heads.

35

A DAY IN THE LIFE
OF A PEDIATRICIAN

It is still dark as I get up before my house awakens with the clatter of the family's morning rituals. My three kids are still sleeping as I close their doors to keep them from hearing me make coffee and pull out some mugs. Bernadette will be rising soon, probably just as I am leaving for the hospital. I am on call, which means I have to go to the hospital to do "rounds," seeing the newborn babies and inpatients that belong to our practice. Today I have two newborns to see before getting to the office for my regular workday of seeing patients from nine to five, or longer.

As I leave, the house remains dark. Bernadette is just rising to start her day, as I say goodbye and head off to the hospital. I sip my coffee out of an aluminum thermos in the car, just finishing it as I enter the hospital parking lot. Up on the third floor, the nursery holds about fifteen newborns. Two are waiting for me to examine for the first time.

By coincidence, both babies were born to mothers over forty years of age. The babies were the first for each family. My exams find both babies to be healthy, so I leave the nursery to talk to the mothers. This is my routine. I familiarize myself with the baby's record and examine the baby before talking to the mother.

The first mother I see is forty-three and very nervous about having her first baby, a girl. She expresses concern about the baby's ability to nurse since in their first night together, the baby did not latch on very well. I explain that nursing doesn't come right away for a new mother or new baby. "Babies are sluggish for the first day or so," I tell her. "As they become more interested on the second or third day, your milk will start coming in." I tell her there are several hurdles to get through in the first couple of weeks, including sore nipples and difficulty latching on, but things get easier in the second week.

I tell her to expect the baby to lose some weight before getting back to its birth weight, no sooner than two weeks of age. "That's usually plenty of time for babies and mothers to get used to nursing. Don't give up," I tell her. "Try for two weeks and you'll see things get better." She seems somewhat satisfied. I answer other questions about the umbilical cord and bathing, and I see her relax more as we speak. As I start to leave I see the tension coming back. She doesn't want me to leave. I reassure her that the nurses will help her, and I'll see her in my office within a week.

The second baby is also a healthy baby girl. Her mother is forty-two years old. Like the first mother, the second mother intends on nursing her baby. The family is of Brazilian descent, and the mother speaks little English. I wonder how much she understands when I speak to her. She appears nervous, but I don't know whether it is over having her first baby or having me, a white male doctor, talking to her about things that in her culture are dealt with among women only. Perhaps the nervousness is only due to the language barrier. I reassure her that her baby is healthy.

I ask the same questions about the feedings and care of her newborn. She answers all my questions with "Fine" or "Okay." I leave wondering whether she would get the same support for her nursing as the first mother. I don't think she is willing to really engage me if she is having nursing issues because of the language and cultural barriers. She seems to understand the support I am offering, but I bet she is going to rely more on friends in her community than on any nurses or lactation consultants I can offer. Despite these misgivings, it's time to move on to my office. I still have a full day ahead.

ON TO THE OFFICE

When I arrive at my office, my first patient is already waiting. A football player hurt his hand at practice the evening before and it swelled up overnight. The boy hit his hand against a teammate's helmet, and now he's afraid it might be broken. He's concerned the injury might force him to miss Saturday's big game. His hand looks fractured to me. I tell him I hope I'm wrong, but I think it's broken. I say that if it's broken he probably can't play for a couple of weeks, but he says he doesn't care, he'll play anyway. I send him to X-ray. We'll continue the discussion when I get a call from X-ray later.

My next patient is a routine check-up for a two-month-old boy. The mother seems happy to see me. She smiles when she sees how much weight her baby has gained. I can sense the pride that comes to mothers when they nurse their babies to good health and growth. She asks some questions about congestion and sleep. She's happy her boy is more restful and less cranky in the evenings lately than he was during the first few weeks. He seems to be settling into life. His exam is perfect. His mother sheds a few tears when he gets his first full set of shots. Overall the visit is pleasant, friendly, and full of good news.

At this point I have a couple of calls on my "call-back phone list." One is about a child with green stools. This is normal for babies, so I believe the parents only need reassurance. The other is from the Department of Social Services about an investigation into a family I care for. This call takes longer than expected. D.S.S. is concerned about abuse and neglect. I know the family and have my own concerns. There is conflict between the mother and father, which creates a stressful environment for the kids. I thought the family needed support, but D.S.S. removing the kids would be too disruptive.

The social worker agrees, so we resolve the questions with mutual satisfaction after a fifteen-minute discussion.

I must get back to my office patients. Now I have two sick patients waiting. The first is a boy with a sore throat. This is very common, especially during school epidemics of strep throat. We have days where our positive strep tests far outnumber the negative. We have two tests for strep. One test gives a result in five minutes with over ninety percent accuracy. The other is an overnight culture that is one hundred percent accurate. We do both tests just to be sure we uncover all our patients who have the illness.

Of all sore throats caused by bacteria and viruses, strep throat is virtually the only one we can treat. This morning, though my patient's throat is quite red, his test is negative. I tell the mother we will double-check with the overnight culture. For the boy I suggest Tylenol and cool liquids. I could tell as the mother leaves that she wishes there were more I could do for his aching throat.

The second patient is an asthmatic, but the mother doesn't know it yet. He has been seen for wheezing and bronchitis at least three previous times. Wheezing is a particular noise we hear in the lungs with a stethoscope. It implies there is a narrowing of the bronchial tubes usually due to a viral infection or allergies. Many physicians call the first two or three wheezing events in a child "bronchitis." But after a child has had wheezing several times as a result of colds, it is apparent the child has a tendency toward wheezing. The tendency is called asthma or reactive airway disease. Many parents react strongly to the "asthma" label, but it is one of the most common diagnoses in pediatrics.

The wheezing boy I see this morning is in for the fourth time in as many months. It is time to talk about treatment and prevention. Despite my reassurances, his mother leaves concerned that her son has a bad chronic illness. I'll cover more about asthma with the mother on the boy's follow-up visit next week. It is hard to explain everything in one visit. Despite its ominous reputation, asthma can be well-cared for today. It is not as scary a diagnosis as it used to be.

Next, I see two children with ear infections — the most common reason for visits to pediatricians' offices in the U.S. Ear infections are caused by bacteria that take advantage of the fluid collecting in children's ears during colds. The infections are usually treated easily, but the fluid accumulated in children's ears takes a long time to go away — usually four to six weeks after a cold or infection. The two patients this morning have simple ear infections and are easily treated. I'll check their ears for fluid in two weeks.

My next check-up is a six-year-old girl who is very afraid at the doctor's office. As I enter, she sits huddled close to her mother with tears streaming down her face. However, she has little to fear for this visit. She is up-to-date on her immunizations and doesn't need any shots, which is the primary cause of fear in our office. Despite this reassurance, the girl stays close to her mother with a look of distrust on her face. I bring out my toys and spread them on the table and start to ignore her. As her mother and I discuss her health, the daughter relaxes and plays with *Toy Story* characters.

The visit goes smoothly. The girl is in good health except for one thing. She is overweight. Her mother tells me the five things she will eat — macaroni, French fries, grilled cheese, cereal, and cheeseburgers. I emphasize that her daughter should not select her own diet. I push for the needed three fruits and three vegetables per day. And, as usual, I press the mother to reduce the four hours per day her daughter spends in front of the TV and computer screen. The daughter returns to a pout and cries as we discuss these issues. I suggest a weight check next month.

Weight is a very sensitive topic at any age. The subject tends to make parents and kids alike defensive. Often there are feelings of blame associated with weight. Parents almost always blame themselves if their child is overweight. Despite these strong feelings about the issue, no illness has increased so dramatically as obesity in my twenty-two years of practice. We now face enormous numbers of enormous kids. No matter how sensitive a subject, we doctors need to confront this illness as much as possible. The health of the next generation is certain to be worse if we don't.

Before I leave the exam room, I reassure this mother that the epidemic of pediatric obesity is just beginning. It is a cultural problem and not hers alone, I tell her.

Before I see my next patient a nurse needs me to answer a question, and a secretary has two calls for me. One call is from a pharmacy needing a clarification on a prescription. The other is from radiology with the result of my first patient's hand X-ray. I clarify the prescription and take the call from X-ray. His hand is broken. He has what is called a "boxer's fracture," where the hand is broken just below the knuckle, such as a boxer might sustain from landing a punch. He needs to be seen by orthopedics and receive a cast, and his ability to play in Saturday's game is doubtful. I speak to his mother about the results. In her voice I can tell she is hesitant about telling him the results. He'll be upset. He lives for football.

By now three patients are waiting. The first is a boy who is having trouble in school. He can't seem to stay on track because he is distracted most of the time. An evaluation by the school suggests he has Attention Deficit and Hyperactivity Disorder. After discussing his schooling with his mother, I start to become convinced of the same diagnosis. I suggest that we evaluate him further by surveying some teachers and both parents through a set of questionnaires about his behavior. The mother agrees, but says that if he has ADHD, she doesn't want to use drugs to treat it. I suggest that we meet again to go over the results of the questionnaires. I lay some foundation about treatment by giving her some statistics about treatment versus non-treatment. I also provide information about the safety and benefits of medications for ADHD. We agree to meet in two weeks to go over the results of the questionnaires.

I'm seeing my next patient with an ear infection when I am interrupted to see a child who fell down a few steps an hour and a half ago. The mother thought he only received a small bump, but then he vomited three times in a half hour. He looks a little out of it, pale and glassy-eyed. I quickly arrange for him to be seen at the emergency room and get a CAT scan. Our testing often ends up to be much ado about nothing, but this boy has the right symptoms for a severe injury. We hope that it is only a concussion. Later, I find out that after causing plenty of worry and anxiety for his parents, the boy's test comes back negative for any internal bleeding. Many times in medicine we have to create more anxiety before we relieve all of it!

At this point, I should be at lunch. But I still have to see a couple of patients. After I see them, I eat my brown-bag lunch while making phone calls and writing up patient charts. By the end of my lunch hour, I have caught up enough to be ready for the afternoon. This is how I spend most of my lunch hours.

A Busy Afternoon

My afternoon starts with a teenage girl who complains of a swollen foot. She wonders if she sprained it. She says she wakes feeling stiff in the morning and has noticed swelling over other joints. I explain to her that the ankle swelling is unlikely due to a sprain. I ask her about whether there are people in her family with arthritis. There are.

She begins to look worried. I describe the testing we will do, and then do the tests. When I send her home, I know she'll worry about whether she has arthritis until the results come back and we know for sure. (Two days later I'll call her to relay the bad news that she has arthritis. I'll refer her to a specialist.)

My afternoon proceeds like the morning. I move from check-up to sick patients and, though I keep moving, I inevitably fall behind. If someone needs to talk longer I always give them the time. All afternoon I am interrupted by calls from specialists I need to speak to, and pharmacies and patients who need answers. I field calls from parents, too. One asks about a penis that "doesn't look right." Others worry about children who won't take their medicines. After school lets out, our office gets busy with cases of strep throat, ear infections, and asthma.

One mother who has brought her child in, asks me to check her ears, too, since she has no insurance. In another case, I need to start a suicidal teenage girl on antidepressant drugs because she can't get in to see her psychiatrist for weeks. A mother shows me her rash to save a trip to her own doctor. A nervous child with warts needs extra attention from me and some numbing of her skin before I treat her warts. A tall overweight middle school girl complains of headaches she gets every day at school. A ten-year-old boy comes in to be treated for bedwetting. A sixteen-year-old boy in foster care is brought in so I can help place him in a drug treatment facility, but there are none in my state for minors. Sometimes I'm amazed at the variety of medical challenges I take care of in one day.

By the end of the afternoon, physical and mental fatigue begin to settle in. I start to look at the clock to see how much longer I have to keep up my energy to provide the best service for my patients. Things are winding down when I go to see my last patient.

When I walk into the exam room, the mother glares at me and lets me have it. Her nine-year-old daughter sits happily on the exam table, but the mother is far from happy. "How come I had to wait a half hour?" she asks. "Couldn't your office staff let us know how far behind you are? I think a half hour is too long for a nine-year-old to be kept waiting!"

I try to explain how I give everyone enough time and that it is hard for staff to judge how much time I may take with a patient. I tell her I don't like being kept waiting either, but I think a half hour wait for a doctor's visit is fairly reasonable. I explain that I have waited that long at dentist, doctor, and orthodontist offices, but none of my explanations satisfy her.

I turn to the child and end up with an endearing encounter with this cute nine-year-old while her mother scowls in the corner with arms folded. The girl needs no shots, but one blood test. My testing in our office lab shows she isn't suffering from anemia, a common affliction for which we screen all children. This girl only needs a follow-up appointment in a year. I finish seeing patients a half-hour overtime and return to my desk. I have kept up on most of my calls but have one left. It is a call I have been dreading.

I need to call the mother of an eight-month-old with an unknown neurological problem to tell her the results of an MRI. "MRI" stands for Magnetic Resonance Imaging and refers to a test that uses magnetic waves to explore the inner anatomy. In this case, the MRI was used to examine the little boy's head. The results showed severe brain damage and a likelihood that the baby would progressively lose neurologic function. This is heartbreaking news. I have saved this until the end of my afternoon because I know I'll need time to talk. I can't be pressured to get to my next patient. Now, with the office quieting down, nurses and secretaries leaving, it's time to place the call.

I tell her the results. I am trying to be gentle, but there is nothing positive about the report. She cries through most of the conversation. The baby has an appointment with a neurology specialist later in the week. I tell her to call me with any questions or for support. We speak for a time while I try to answer her questions. She thanks me for calling and for giving her support. My day is done.

In the end, I have seen thirty-one patients and answered twelve phone calls. It's been a pretty average day by the numbers, but particular cases make some days worse than others. This has been a hard day. I've had to handle a number of serious issues. Some of my patients and parents faced new physical and emotional health concerns. They looked to me for treatment, reassurance, and advice. I've tried my best. I am tired, and now it is time to go home to my family.

36

THE BEST PEDIATRIC LESSON: KIDS OF MY OWN

The best experience I've had as a pediatrician was becoming a parent. As a new parent I had to experience all the advice I had given parents.

"Just let them cry it out."

"You have to show them who is in charge."

These are just a couple of the many lines I used before having kids — lines that are not in my repertoire today. I learned as much about pediatrics from being a parent as I did during my residency.

My son was born in Chicago. I was at the Cubs-Pirates game at Wrigley Field when my wife called me after the third inning. He was born late in the evening after a long time pushing. (Hey, kid, couldn't I have stayed for the whole game?) During the hospital stay he was an angel — sleeping, eating, peeing, and pooping — doing just what a baby is supposed to do. He slept so solidly that we spent most of our time at the hospital trying to wake him so we could feed him or show him off.

After two days we got him home and everything went downhill. The day we got home he cried all night long. Every day for three months he would have a crying fit lasting an hour to three hours straight. He couldn't fall asleep without crying for at least an hour, and any little sound would wake him up to start crying all over again. We held him constantly. We lived in a tiny bungalow at the time — our first home. It had five rooms: three downstairs and two upstairs. There was no escaping the sound of a baby crying.

During the first weeks of his life, Bernadette questioned my advice regularly. Despite my answers, she often preferred getting expert advice from our friend, Laura, who was my colleague and our pediatrician. The crying problem persisted for weeks, and it became clear we had a colicky baby.

"So what causes colic?" Bernadette asked. "How long does it last? What's the best treatment?"

Somehow my advice to my wife, "You just have to ride it out, it goes away," didn't suffice. Even I didn't buy that advice. I wondered what was going on with this colicky kid. I wanted to know why it happened and what we could do about it.

That stimulated a minor research study for me. I found that ten percent of babies are colicky and, congratulations, we were one of the grand prize winners. These kids tend to have fussy times, usually toward evening. They often seem gassy and pull up their legs in apparent discomfort. Nobody really knows the cause.

What we do know is that the crying periods peak at six weeks of age and usually end by the twelfth week. There are many suggestions about what to do with a crying, colicky baby: change formula, use Mylicon drops, drive them in a car for a while, use a car simulator that attaches to the crib, change formulas again, change your diet if you're a nursing mom, keep them close, put them down, put ice on their belly, put warm clothes on their belly, use a snuggly, give them chamomile tea, and so on and so on.

The main thing is to make sure you have many hands on deck to share the work. Take the bits of advice that work for you. And most of all, relax. The symptoms *will* go away in three months. My wife says you just have to give up on the idea that you can stop the crying.

My cousin visited in the middle of our colicky period. She later recalled that we had our son in constant movement. Bernadette used the rocker effectively. I was doing more with a rain dance kind of bounce/walk.

We rode it out and eventually it did go away. Although he continued to cry himself to sleep every night and at every nap for more than eighteen months, he would then sleep well. This was only lesson one for me as parent-pediatrician. In the coming years, I would learn about discipline, sleep, temper tantrums, lies, aggression, TV, school issues, and how to parent a teenager. Parenting is a learning experience, and the lessons come every step along the way — even for a pediatrician.

37

COMEDY IN PRACTICE

I've learned over the years that there is nothing more important in practice than making patients comfortable to see you, and nothing works better at making patients comfortable than laughter.

Making kids laugh can be easy at times, though the fear that comes with going to the doctor can make it difficult. I enjoy having a sense of humor and using it in practice. Sometimes it is appreciated. Sometimes it's not. Nonetheless, I try. At times I feel like I could have been a comedian for the under-seven crowd, but I don't think there's a big market for that.

Maybe I could do birthday parties! Bring a pediatrician to your birthday!

Occasionally my humor is directed to the parents. During school vacation seasons, parents often come into my office and ask things like "Can my baby fly?"

or "I just wanted to know if my baby can fly?" Or else they ask, "Do you think my baby can fly?" Of course I know what they mean. Their vacation destination requires that they travel by plane, and they want to know if their child is healthy enough to go. But that's not what they ask.

"What makes you think she can't fly?" begins my line of Joe Friday-like questioning.

"She's just getting over a cold," they'll typically respond.

"Well, could she fly before her cold?"

"Yes, she flew to California last year."

"Well — let's see if she can do it now. How does she usually take off? Should I launch her or should you?"

Many times I've felt like balancing the baby on the palm of my hand and saying, "I'll toss her and see if she stays aloft."

Of course, I never have, and I usually take their concern seriously and provide reassurance. After the exam I usually share my humor with the parent. Sometimes they appreciate it.

During most visits I save my material for the kids. It's much easier getting them to laugh with an unusual handshake or simple magic trick. I don't know how many quarters I have taken out of children's ears.

However, the best comedy usually comes from the kids themselves. One boy came to me to reassess his allergies. He was a very precocious six-year-old. He told me all about his symptoms. He told me which medicines were working and which weren't. He was so chatty his mother couldn't get a word in edgewise.

His mother and I sat listening to him go on and on. Even after examining his ears, nose, and throat he still wasn't done. Finally, he ended with, "Anyway, Doctor, I don't care which medicine you want to try next but whatever you do don't give me that Viagra stuff."

His mother and I couldn't keep it together. After a good laugh, I reassured him that I wasn't going to use that "Viagra stuff."

Humor is an important part of my practice. If you keep your mind open to it, there is something everyday in a pediatric office that will make you laugh.

38

MANAGING DEATH WITH RESPECT, DIGNITY, AND LOVE

Most of my practice deals with thriving and growing children, so I have not often encountered death. But during my early years in medicine, I encountered children's deaths several times. I had the two cases of Sudden Infant Death Syndrome in Italy and Neal's death back in Washington.

I encountered other deaths during my residency, particularly with cancer patients. I came to learn through experience that a proper death is something we in medicine have to help create. Hospitals have not always incorporated this into their thinking. Some people in medicine are beginning to recognize this more, which is one reason why the hospice movement has grown. A proper death includes respect, dignity, and love.

One death during my residency that didn't happen

that way involved a two-year-old child suffering from AIDS. The girl, whose name was Mindy, was born prematurely and contracted the virus through a blood transfusion. At age two she lay dying in the intensive care unit at Bethesda Naval Hospital. Her father wanted her transferred to a nearby children's hospital because he thought they could do more for her. We told him nothing more could be done, that her lungs were full of fluid and she was suffering from severe pneumonia. It was her third or fourth battle with pneumonia. This time she was in a coma.

In that era of AIDS treatment during the early 1980s there was no hope after so many pneumonias. The best hope was that Mindy would die in peace with her family and friends close by.

Mindy's father won out in his wish to transfer his daughter. The children's hospital to which she was transferred did all they could, meaning more medication and aggressive ICU care. Mindy even received a bolt in her head to relieve pressure, a gruesome last-resort procedure. She died lying in a bed bloated beyond recognition with tubes in every orifice. I'm sure the ICU team tried their best to help the family process such a horrible death. But who could help process that? Those last visions of Mindy must be etched in her parents' minds. Months later her mother told me, "It wasn't my daughter — the daughter I knew — in that bed."

Mindy's parents divorced shortly after her death. Her father couldn't face the fact that there was nothing that could have been done. He felt that someone, somewhere, missed a step that would have saved his daughter. Our society has been taught to have those expectations. It is too bad that people have not learned that during those last moments of life, dignity, respect, and love are more essential in some cases than extreme life-saving measures.

Death doesn't have to be so horribly sad. At times it can even be beautiful. It may not seem that way at the time, especially to close family members, but if a family experiences a "beautiful" death, it helps them process that death more easily and mourn more peacefully. Over time, they can look back and see the beauty. Neal's death had more beauty for his mother than Mindy's death had for her mom. It is the last visions of their children's deaths these mothers have to live with forever.

39

BIG OFFICE, SMALL OFFICE

I needed to see my doctor one day last year. The experience gave me an interesting look at the hierarchy in today's medical world. It started at my office, which is in an older medical office building. Our six exam rooms are shared by four doctors. Our two offices each have two desks. In all, we have two computers and four phones. The point is: we're crowded. This meager space fits our budget, even though we serve a large number of patients and employ four doctors.

When I went for the first time to my internal medicine primary care doctor, I was struck by a familiar theme. I knew him years ago when he was in training. Today, he practices by himself. He is also in a medical office building. He has a small waiting room with about five or six chairs. His registration area is part of a hallway.

He practices full-time but must make time available for early morning and evening meetings because he is part of the management board of the local hospital. What was surprising to me was seeing him practicing out of such tiny quarters when he is so high up on the hospital hierarchy.

Before the exam, we caught up a little. We talked about how practice life was going, and he gave me his opinion on the direction of our industry. "As long as pharmaceuticals and high-tech medicine keep getting more of the health care dollars, practitioners like us are going to struggle more and more," he said.

After the exam, I made an appointment for an MRI on my neck. When I went for the MRI a few days later, I was stunned by the MRI office, which was in a new medical office building The office was so impressive with its tall ceilings, nice paintings, and upscale furniture that I felt like I was walking into a downtown law office. The waiting room was spacious, with coffee, television, and a pile of recent magazines. When it was my turn, a technician showed me to a dressing/waiting area to change my clothes for the test. Another set of chairs, a television, and magazines were there for my pleasure. I had my test, changed, and left.

I recalled my doctor's words about high-tech medicine. His words weren't news to me, but to see the obvious difference between our primary care offices and the MRI office really made me think. No MRI machine has ever cured a patient. In fact, it is safe to say the results of most MRI tests are normal. Many are not even needed in the first place, but are ordered by doctors just to make sure they don't miss anything. It's part of the "cover your ass" attitude in the litigious world of medicine today. It is also fair to say that MRI testing and other testing like it are overused. There are certainly times when they are necessary, but medical technology has never been used discriminately. Should it be used more conservatively? Should we be spending such a large amount of health care dollars on MRIs?

There are only so many health care dollars to go around. The more we spend on MRIs and other expensive tests, the less we spend on primary care physicians, forcing them to see more patients to maintain their income.

I am not looking for a bigger, better office for myself. But as primary care struggles to maintain the key trusting relationships between doctor and patient that lead to good quality health care, we need to start answering these questions. It is not about office space. It is about where insurance dollars are going.

40

KAWASAKI

A couple of years ago while practicing at a health center in the Boston area, I examined a seven-year-old boy with a sore throat. Normally for children with sore throats, we do a throat culture in which we use a Q-tip to take a sample from inside the child's throat. The throat sample is placed in an incubator overnight, which makes any bacteria present grow quickly and become easy to identify by the next day. On this boy, I did a throat culture and sent the family on their way. I advised the child to drink loads of liquids, and I told them I would contact them with the throat culture results.

After a day or two, I called with the culture results, and the mother told me her son was no better than when I had seen him. In fact, she said his neck had swelled even larger. I told her the culture was negative, not showing any presence of the type of bacteria we can treat with antibiotics. That meant her son likely had a virus for which there is no treatment, and he would have to recover on his own. I instructed her to watch him for now, but to call me if things got worse.

The next day she called. Her son had looked worse when he had gotten up that morning. Now both his eyes were bloodshot. I could hear the concern in her voice. It was still likely to be a virus, but I told her to bring him in again anyway.

Something didn't feel right to me.

When I saw the boy, he had terribly bloodshot eyes, his neck was puffy and swollen, his hands were peeling, and his lips and throat were beet red. I no longer thought of this as a simple viral infection. I had some ideas about what it might be, but I was perplexed by his appearance.

I had never seen a case like this in all my years of practice, twelve at that time. There was something in the back of my head about what it was, but I couldn't think of it clearly. I excused myself from the exam room to talk to a colleague about the case. I told her how the boy's culture was negative and how he looked today. My colleague is a brilliant clinician, and when we discussed the case she immediately put it all together.

"Of course, Kawasaki's is a big mimicker of strep throat," she said.

"That's it!!" I said. "That's what he has!"

Kawasaki's disease is a mysterious illness whose exact cause is known. Its symptoms include sore throat, conjunctivitis, swollen glands, swollen mucous membranes, and peeling hands and feet. Kawasaki's disease can have devastating consequences if left untreated, including irreversible coronary artery damage. It is rare, however, and most pediatricians see only a couple of cases of Kawasaki's disease in their careers.

I went back into the exam room and explained what we had concluded. We referred the boy immediately to Children's Hospital in Boston. The rheumatologist who saw him there called to tell me what a "great pickup" I had made. A great pickup is doctors' lingo for a good clinical diagnosis. The rheumatologist had started the boy with an intravenous line of immunoglobulin therapy. For unknown reasons, an infusion of immunoglobulins usually stops the devastating effects Kawasaki's disease has on the body. Immunoglobulins are proteins in the body that fight disease. Immunoglobulin therapy uses a broad range of these disease-fighting proteins to treat illness.

The immunoglobulin therapy was the main treatment for the boy's illness, and within forty-eight hours he was perfectly fine.

The boy and his family lived in my town, and I bumped into his parents at a park months later. They said they had told many people the story of their son's unique illness, and they had sung my praises to all of them. I thanked them, but went away thinking, "Thank God I listened to the mother and brought him back in." The parents didn't know how scared and worried I had been when I didn't know what his diagnosis was. They knew I shared their concern, but they didn't know I needed help to figure out what was ailing their boy.

I was thankful that I could so easily turn to my col-

league for help. The big lesson for me was how important it is to listen to the words and the urgency behind
them when assessing a mother's concern for her sick
child. That's what the family thanked me for most —
listening. The other lesson for me was that even after
years of practice, I was still learning. At every stage of
my career it has been so important to know my limits,
and know when to get help from colleagues. In medicine two heads are often better than one.

41

NEW MOTHERS

I've found there aren't many experiences more fun than helping new parents with their first child. Many pediatricians and their staff roll their eyes and say things like, "Oh brother, these first-time moms . . ." but I enjoy them. They're clueless. Before the baby is born, there is no way for them to anticipate what it is like to have and care for their first baby.

Nowadays, new moms come for a visit having read two to five books during their pregnancy. Only later do they discover that all that knowledge is useless after the first moment the baby is placed in their arms. It's impossible to remember and follow all the information in all those books. The biggest problem is the baby has never read the books, so he doesn't follow them either.

It is amazing that once they have that little person, born out of their own belly, there is an automatic numbing of the mind. I am not saying that just about women or mothers. It is not meant to be derogatory. It is just such a powerful event to be changed from "expectant mother" to "mother" or "expectant father" to "father." It is an understandably mind-numbing experience.

I love the looks of sheer joy and anticipation on the faces of the new parents. Their eyes are tired but bright, and the baby is the whole focus of their life. Weeks earlier they could have been watching the World Series, doing their taxes, or going out for Thai food, but that world is soon forgotten.

I have asked several couples after months of seeing them with their baby whether they can remember a time when they did not have a baby. Almost all of them can barely remember their world prior to the baby being part of it. Their conversations have changed from stock markets, TV shows, or sports to how many poops there were today.

I love showing the parents how to do things better. Often first-time parents will gingerly handle the baby and then not even handle it successfully. Then I'll pick the baby up freely and easily as they watch with amazement that the baby doesn't break when I do it.

I love answering all the questions.

"Is it normal for the baby to—"

"Is it normal for the baby to—"

"Is it normal for the baby to—"

The answer is almost always, "Yes."

I also love giving them things to anticipate. They think I am brilliant when they come back to the office and say, "You were right, Doctor, the very next week he started grabbing things."

The hardest part is when I have to tell a new parent there is something wrong with the baby. It almost doesn't matter if it's a hangnail or a heart murmur. All parents hope their child is perfect, but unfortunately that can't always be.

Fortunately, most things are minor, though with new parents even minor things can't be treated as such. A heavy dose of reassurance is always required.

It is always more joyful to tell new parents their child is in perfect health. Often during a mother's first visit to me with her baby I get the opportunity to tell her all is well. The joy and excitement I see in her eyes is always touching.

42

JUDGING A MOTHER'S LOVE

I have been called to court for many child abuse and neglect cases over the years, but one very tragic case sticks out in my mind.

I took care of two girls who were born to a drug-addicted mother. One girl was two years old and the other was six months. Both children had been in foster care and had recently returned to the mother's custody when they started coming to see me.

The mother was in her late twenties, but looked much older. She was extremely apathetic. The most bothersome thing was that she never seemed to pay attention to what was going on with her daughters. She was often distant. It was as if the girls were a burden that got in the way of her life. She often came to the office with a social worker, who tried to help her pull things together. The two girls were very small for their ages, poorly dressed, and ill-kept. I saw them frequently for ear infections over a two- to three-month period.

I remember one visit particularly well. The mother and social worker brought the two girls into the office. When I went into the exam room, the mother was in a corner flipping through a magazine while the two kids sat precariously on the exam table. As I walked in, the social worker was telling the mother she should watch the children on the table. The mother replied gruffly and indifferently, "They're fine."

I asked what the children's problems were. The social worker told me the mother had called her and said the kids were sick. This time, I asked the mother directly what their problems were.

"They both have colds," she said, hardly looking up from her magazine.

I could tell she would provide me with little information, so I went right into the exam. When I examined the two-year-old, I found that both her ears were draining pus. "Her ears are full of pus," I told the mother.

"What do you mean — really?" she said. "I clean her ears. I didn't notice anything."

I examined the younger child. She also had pus coming from both ears. The mother was now up from her seat and the magazine had been thrown aside. "They can't have another ear infection," she said. " I didn't see any pus."

I showed her the children's ears. The pus was easily noticeable. It had been there long enough to form a crust below the children's ears, which told me it had been there for several hours.

The Department of Social Services, the state agency that cares for children at risk from abuse and neglect, had been heavily involved with the two girls for a while. The mother's boyfriend, who was the girls' father, lived with them but hardly ever came to my appointments. The social worker told me he was not helpful at all in caring for the children. Obviously, there were serious questions about the ability of both these parents to care for their girls. After the appointment, the social worker and I spoke with D.S.S., and a court date was set up. Custody of the children would be decided in court.

When the court date arrived, I was called from my office and spent the afternoon waiting for my turn to testify. I was called as a witness for the state. The two children were each represented by a lawyer, and each parent was represented by a separate lawyer since they were not married. So there were five lawyers on this one case: four defense lawyers and one state attorney representing D.S.S.

When I was finally brought to the stand, I remained standing after being sworn in. I stood on a witness stand that was surrounded by a curved railing and overlooked the tables where the five lawyers and the parents sat.

The state's attorney started the questioning and asked me to go over the important medical aspects of the case. After I talked for a short time, the state's lawyer asked the judge whether I could be declared an "expert witness." Not fully understanding what this meant, I felt like *I* wanted to object. I didn't want to be declared an "expert" in anything — especially in what would be asked of me next.

The judge approved my new "expert witness" status without objection from the defense. The state's attorney then asked me about the children's mother.

"Was she a loving mother?"

"I object." "I object." "I object." "I object," echoed in the courtroom as all four defense lawyers rose to their feet. They all seemed to talk at once.

"Who is he to judge another's love?" one said. "Is he an expert in love?" said another. "How is he going to be defining 'loving'?" said a third. "How is he as a physician going to judge how much this woman loves her daughters?" said a fourth.

The questions rang out before the gavel sounded to restore order. The judge sat thoughtfully for a moment and then said, "I, for one, would like to hear his opinion on this. After all, he has witnessed many different family relationships over the years, haven't you, Doctor?"

I nodded numbly.

"Let's hear what he has to say," said the judge.

All eyes in the courtroom turned to me. I was being asked to judge a mother's love as that mother sat ten feet away. Five lawyers, two parents, two social workers, the court reporter, and the judge waited for my response.

I turned slowly from the judge, whom I had been looking to for a reprieve from this sentence, to the lawyer who had asked me to play Dear Abby. My eyes moved from the floor to the lawyer and back again as I thought about the question. I finally said what I felt in my gut.

"No, she is not a loving mother."

Wails and cries rang out from the mother. The father stared daggers at me. The four lawyers rose again in objection. The judge gaveled the proceedings back to order.

"I would like to hear him finish," the judge said firmly. "Everyone sit back down."

I went on to explain that the mother seemed disinterested in her children. I described the visit where she didn't even realize the children had pus draining from their ears, and I spoke about her indifferent demeanor in the office. As a result of my testimony, the judge removed the children from the parents' custody and transferred them to foster care under D.S.S. supervision. Understanding my time constraints, the judge allowed me to leave before the proceedings were over. Thankfully, I didn't have to face the parents in the court hallways.

I continued to see the two little girls on visits to my office while they were in foster care. Within six months we diagnosed both of them with AIDS. This was around 1990, a time when AIDS was still very deadly. The case ended tragically. Both little girls died while in foster care before they were five years old. It was a very sad experience overall. For me it was the only time I was asked to be an expert on someone else's love. I hope it's the last.

43

NICE TO MEET YOU

One morning at work, I was on my way back from grabbing vaccines from the refrigerator for a patient when I noticed one of my medical assistants struggling with a baby at a weighing scale. The assistant gave me a look I won't forget. "H-E-L-P" was written in her eyes and eyebrows.

I looked down at the baby she was weighing. He was blue in color and struggling to breathe. I dropped my vaccines and grabbed the baby. I pulled his jaw forward to open his airway. It helped a little. The baby looked a bit pinker. With the child cradled in my arms and my fingers still holding his jaw out, I went into an empty exam room and called for oxygen and an ambulance.

I asked my assistant to get the baby's mother, who was waiting down the hall in another exam room. She came in as we were strapping the oxygen mask on the boy's face. I asked her what was going on with the baby, telling her that he had just turned blue while being weighed.

"Well that's the problem," she said. "He's blue when I lay him down."

When the ambulance arrived, I told the emergency workers that I needed to ride in the ambulance holding the child with his jaw jutted forward and the oxygen on. I told them we would need equipment standing by in case it was necessary to intubate the baby, a process by which a tube is placed down the throat to keep the airway open.

"We need to get to the hospital fast," I said.

The baby's mother traveled with me in the ambulance. "What's your name anyway?" she thought to ask midway to the hospital.

"I'm Doctor Orr," I said.

"I'm Joan Conti," she said. "And you are holding my son, Sam."

"Nice to meet you," we both said.

I said hopefully the next time we met it would be in better circumstances. We arrived at the hospital within ten minutes, and within an hour the boy was taken to emergency surgery for a peritonsilar abscess, which is a collection of pus behind one of the tonsils that can block the airway.

I still don't know what happened to the patient who was waiting for those shots when I saw the blue baby on the scale. I assume my colleagues filled in for me.

As far as my sick little friend, I saw Sam and his mother again many times. I took care of him for years and later his baby brother, too. The boys had many serious issues. They tended to be acutely sick frequently and had some chronic problems as well. After that first ride in the ambulance, the mother and I had a special bond.

Mrs. Conti had a trust in me that never faltered. Her second son was born prematurely and seemed to catch everything Sam brought home. I was meticulous in my care of him and she knew I would be. I have enjoyed many great relationships with mothers whose children were in my care, but that was the only one that started in such a dramatic way.

44

JUST BE THERE

A mother brought her two boys in for a sick visit. One was three years old and the other had just turned one. Both had colds, and the mother seemed very distraught. I could hardly believe she was that upset over her sons' colds. Something else was wrong.

When I asked her if everything was all right, she broke down in tears and told me that she was so busy because she was trying to get doctor appointments for her mother. She was debating her mother's care with different medical specialists, but the consensus was that her mother was dying of cancer and had a very short time to live. She and her mother had been estranged for years and had only in the past few years reconciled their differences. Her mother was just starting to enjoy her grandchildren. Then she got cancer.

The mother was upset because her life was too

busy caring simultaneously for her sick children and her sick mother. She didn't know whether her mother should get another opinion, and she was struggling with too many difficult questions. Were there other scans her mother should get to further define the cancer? Were there other therapies they weren't thinking of? What was the next thing she should do for her mother? After all, something had to be done because her mother was dying, she told me in what eventually became a tirade.

When she was done, I asked if she wanted my opinion. She said she did. I told her I thought it was time to stop "doing" and her job was now to "be there." I suggested she set up hospice care for her mother, and then just be there to listen and care for her. As a pediatrician, I was taking a risk. I didn't know for sure if anything else could be done for her mother, but I had a feeling it was just time to stop "doing."

I remember her response clearly. It was like a response you see in the movies when the actress says nothing but looks like something just dawned on her. The woman left my office in a pensive state. I could see the wheels turning.

After her mother's death she wrote me a note. She thanked me for my understanding during the trauma of her mother's illness. I guess my gut feeling was correct. It's amazing how much of medicine is following your gut feeling and having the courage to express it. It's also amazing that as we face the inevitable it's so hard for us to stop "doing" things. Sometimes it's better just to be there and witness.

45

SHAKEN

One day many years ago, I was about to go to lunch when my assistant asked me to see a patient for a colleague who was running behind. I was happy to help out.

It was a case of head trauma, which in small children usually means a bump on the head from a fall against a coffee table. I figured it would be a quick case and wouldn't delay my lunch too much.

When I came into the exam room, the mother made a vague comment about the baby bumping his head. It was then that I realized the baby was only six months old.

My eyes fixated on the baby's head. There were lumps. There were bruises. I asked the mother, "How does a six-month-old bump his head?"

The mother was vague once again. "I don't know

how it happened," she said. "Only my husband and I take care of him."

The baby was staring blankly. Both sides of his head were swollen. The swollen parts felt like they had blood in them under the scalp.

The child had been shaken and abused.

After digesting the obvious signs of superficial trauma on the baby, I became concerned about internal trauma. The child needed to get to the hospital quickly for evaluation and possible surgery to stop any internal bleeding. When I told the mother my impressions and told her that I would call an ambulance, she asked to call her husband. I offered my office phone but she instead left the office to use a pay phone.

This was very suspicious. I was concerned she might run away, so while the nurses cared for the baby in the exam room I followed the mother to the pay phone in our lobby downstairs and had security watch her. After all, she had already admitted to me it was either she or her husband who had done this to the baby.

The father worked close by and was there when the ambulance arrived. His wife had informed him of my concerns, and he came storming into my office. "Who did this?" he said. "How could this have happened? Who could have hurt my child like this?"

His angry tirade made me feel as if he were accusing me of hurting the baby. "My wife and I take good care of this baby," he said, glaring at me. "We don't let anybody else take care of our baby."

As the EMTs stabilized the little boy, I pulled the ranting father aside. He was repeating his questions, and his actions helped me reach my own conclusion about who had done this to the baby.

"If it's only you two who care for the boy, it was probably one of you two," I fired back at him. "I am required to report this case to the Department of Social Services." In Massachusetts, state law requires doctors to report suspected child abuse.

In other cases, I have been more tactful in expressing my need to report to D.S.S. But after seeing this poor baby and watching the father's tirade, I had no more tolerance for him or his behavior.

Later that day at the hospital, the father was arrested for assault and attempted murder for hurting his only child. Due largely to my testimony about the baby's trauma and the parents' admission that they were the only ones who cared for the boy, the father was convicted and sent to prison, where he remains twelve years later. When the baby was examined at the hospital, doctors found he had other fractures and retinal hemorrhages, which are bruises behind the eyes that are a sure sign of Shaken Baby Syndrome. After a lengthy hospitalization, the child was placed in foster care. I saw him a couple of times during his recovery. The trauma had slowed his development and he began walking and talking much later than the average child.

No class or training prepared me for cases like that one. Perhaps there is no preparation for that kind of case. From the moment I began providing care to the child, through my deposition for the court case, the sight of the baby's fragile broken head and his vacant stare on my exam table stuck in my head. As pediatricians we see so many normal babies that when we see something so dramatically wrong, we know it right away and the image lingers for a long time. Even today, more than a decade later, I can easily visualize that little boy.

I hope few doctors ever have to experience such a terrible case. There are foundations trying to raise awareness of Shaken Baby Syndrome, including the Matty Eappen Foundation, which was named for a baby in Massachusetts who died after being shaken by his British au pair.[2] With time I hope the work of these foundations decreases the incidence of this awful tragedy.

2. www.mattyeappen.org.

46

SMILES AND HUGS

Years after my first encounter with a victim of Shaken Baby Syndrome, I encountered another.

This time I didn't see the child so soon after the injuries occurred. He was brought to me by his foster mother while he was recovering. The boy was four months old when I started seeing him. His foster mother and I were concerned he would encounter many developmental problems, after suffering severe skull fractures due to Shaken Baby Syndrome at the hands of his birth parents. He had bleeding under the skull caused by vigorous shaking of his head and some bleeding behind his eyes. There was concern that he would never see.

The foster mother was loving and kind. She raised concerns about his vision on her first visit. As I examined him, I agreed with her. The boy didn't focus on anything the way four-month-olds usually do. He didn't hold his head up well either. We both agreed there could be more concerns about his development than just his vision.

I saw him regularly for months, but our concerns didn't subside. We sent him to an ophthalmologist and a neurologist. Based on their assessment, we sent the boy to a school for the blind for early intervention.

As the boy approached one year of age, he started to give us hope. He actually started grabbing things, though his reach was awkward. He would overreach for an object and then come back for it. The way he reached made it unclear whether he was seeing the object or just feeling the air for it. It was also possible that he could see something but his depth perception and focus were way off. Though it still wasn't clear to us whether he was seeing, we started to have hope.

The boy came in for his fifteen-month checkup in the middle of a very busy afternoon. I picked up his chart and darted off toward the exam room. I was unsure what I would find when I opened the door.

When I opened the exam room door, this little blond boy looked up at me, smiled, walked across the room and gave me a big hug around my leg. I was frozen in the moment with my mouth agape. I looked at the foster mother, and both of us had tears in our eyes. We were ecstatic. Not only was he seeing, but he had just learned to walk as well.

There are still many questions left unanswered about his future. He has surprised us so much with his resilience and recovery from early trauma that we don't know when he will stop beating the odds. He has given us so much hope. I just want to sit back and watch him as he grows. I think he's going to be okay.

A long time ago I was taught to believe in miracles. I'm glad he reminded me of that lesson.

47

ANOTHER SPECIAL PATIENT

I've already told the story of Neal, my first special patient. In the last ten years of practice I've had the opportunity to work with another special patient. His name was Mike. Neal and Mike had the same handicaps, including cerebral palsy, spastic quadriplegia, and mental retardation, and they both had the ability to use only basic modes of communication. They were also lucky enough to be cared for by great, loving mothers.

Mike's mother persevered through all of his medical and surgical visits. Through it all she was entirely dedicated to his care. She took only two weeks off each year from caring for his every need. She was responsible for feeding, changing, and medicating her son for over eighteen years.

As was the case with Neal, I once again witnessed

the medical personnel's lack of understanding of the special bond between mothers and their children with special needs. Once Mike underwent orthopedic surgery to loosen tendons in his legs — a common surgery for cerebral palsy patients — he lost some of his already limited ability to communicate. Before surgery he could move his eyes up for "yes" and to the side for "no," but because his intravenous fluids were not managed properly during the surgery he lost even that ability.

When the surgeon was in the hospital, he discussed the case with me and the rest of the medical team. When we got to the topic of the fluid mismanagement, the surgeon was dismissive. "Well, he was damaged anyway," the surgeon said.

It was an appalling response. Mike's mother relied on his ability to communicate with his eyes. It was a cornerstone of their relationship. Every little bit of skill Mike had was important to her. Now this crucial one was gone.

Nevertheless, she persisted in her daily care for Mike until it became more and more difficult to manage him at home. Then she went through an excruciating process of deciding whether to place him in a home. She finally decided to place him in a home for children with such severe disabilities they needed care beyond what their parents could give.

The decision saddened her. She lived for him, and she was completely dedicated to him. Nobody understood how devastating it was for her now that he was no longer at home with her.

Friends said things like: "It must be such a relief" and "You've had such a burden" and "Now you can get on with your life."

I had heard those phrases before. I was happy to have the chance to talk to her and relay my story about my first Neal. I was able to understand her love for her son and reassure her that I knew there was never any "burden" for her.

When we witness families like this, we often feel sympathy for the parents and feel bad for the "burden" they have. Yet the parents of these children may not be experiencing their life that way. It is so important for us to recognize that mothers of special children like these two can love in a special way that is difficult for the rest of us to comprehend. Their love makes them especially dedicated to their children. For them, there is never any "relief" in losing their child.

48

THE USE OF ABUSE

I have never heard this talked about or seen it written about, but I have experienced it many times over the years. I call it the "use of abuse." It's when a father or mother — most often fathers in my experience — accuses their former spouse of child abuse to obtain more custody of their child. The battles over custody are often horrible enough, but using the abuse claim is the lowest of the low in my opinion. It happens more often than you might think.

I can recall three cases off the top of my head. Two of them involved girls with bruises on their shins. In both cases, the fathers brought their daughters into the office repeatedly and claimed the bruises were caused by the girls' violent mothers. Social services were contacted several times, but no one ever found that the mothers had done anything wrong. Still, the accusations kept the mothers on the defensive, especially in court. On a daily basis, they lived in fear that their daughters would pick up a new bruise that would lead to another abuse accusation to social services. Even a fall in the playground could result in a new accusation of abuse.

The third case was even worse. In that case, I had to go to court and testify against "experts" from a teaching hospital. It started with a call from the emergency room of a teaching hospital. A patient of mine was there with his father. The father claimed that the boy, who was not yet a year old, had been dunked in scalding hot water by his mother.

Already well aware of the brutal custody battle between the parents in this case, I told the ER doctor to be careful about blaming the mother for the baby's injuries. Nevertheless, the "child abuse team" from the hospital said it was a burn and the burn was consistent with the father's story.

There was only one problem with the father's version of what happened. The child had had bad diarrhea. I had spoken to the mother and knew this to be true. I saw the child the day after receiving the call from the emergency room of the teaching hospital. The boy had no splash burns. When a child is dunked in scalding water, he often has burns in a splash and splatter pattern up his legs and trunk. On this little boy, the only "burned" area was in the area where diarrhea would contact his skin. Bad diarrhea often causes chemical burns.

In court, the claim of abuse was dismissed because

of my testimony. Still, the mother had already lost some custody time in the process, and now she had to renegotiate for custody time after the claim was dismissed.

In all my experience, I find few things more detestable than people who use their lawyers, their money, and claims of abuse to obtain more custody of their children. The social service system is too taxed already. For it to be tied up with false claims of abuse is a form of abuse in itself.

I am glad to have had relationships with families in situations like these. Because of my investment in their children and in the truth, I have been able to help some parents retain rightful custody of their kids.

49

MIRACLE IN MEXICO

At one point in my career, I examined the service I was providing and decided what I was doing was not enough. I had been volunteering monthly on a medical van for the homeless, but I really wanted to get back to the work I had been doing earlier in my career in places outside the U.S. where the needs were so great that one could make a significant contribution even in a short time.

I thought of my work in the Dominican Republic just before my residency and decided it was time to return to an underdeveloped country. I looked around for opportunities, but my Spanish-language abilities were weak.

As luck would have it, I found a perfect opportunity in a language/volunteer program in Mexico, seventy miles north of Puerto Vallarta. A Mexican-

American doctor developed the program in which participants could study Spanish two days a week and volunteer at a clinic three days a week. The clinic was on the edge of a small city on the road from Puerto Vallarta to Guadalajara. The city itself was all stone and stucco with potholed streets. The clinic was on a hill where the paved road stopped and the dirt road began. It had four to five exam rooms that opened on a courtyard where patients waited. It was a "waiting *courtyard*" instead of a "waiting *room.*"

The clinic was poorly stocked, but the people who worked there did their best with what they had and took great care of the patients. It was obvious that they knew the patients and their families well.

The medical equipment was old, and the shelves held few medicines. I took a picture of the mostly empty pharmacy shelves. The clinic had one nebulizer machine for treating asthmatics. A nebulizer machine has tubing that carries medicated mist to the patient's nose. In the U.S. we put on a clean tubing for each patient. The clinic had one set of tubing, which was old, yellow, and had mold in it. A treatment with that machine and tubing could make some asthmatics worse instead of better.

Such was the state of the clinic. It was this way in part because of its location in a very rural area of Mexico. It was also due to the clinic's independence, and its decision to stay away from government influence and money. Instead, the people who ran the clinic relied on donations and whatever fees they could charge their patients. Despite the poor facilities, the people who worked there provided an incredible service to their community, as evidenced by the popularity of their practice.

We stayed in a small town on the water about five miles away. It took us a half hour to travel from the town where we stayed to the clinic because the road was rocky, unpaved, and potholed. All the doctors, medical students, and nurse practitioners who volunteered at the clinic traveled together in a van from town to the clinic. We stayed at the clinic each day until dark.

My experience at the clinic is best illustrated by excerpts from the journal I kept during the trip.

Monday, November 18

Spent the day at the clinic. Saw a couple of patients with typical colds and ear infections. Had an amazing encounter with a two-month-old who had been born after just thirty-four weeks at six pounds, nine ounces but now weighed only five pounds, one ounce.[3] She was extremely thin with wrinkled skin and muscle wasting. She had an extremely poor suck and deep sunken eyes. Her fontanel was sunken. Her eyes had a blank look and she hung her dry mouth open. She could

3. Healthy babies often lose weight immediately after birth, but should be back to their birth weight and growing within two weeks. This baby, who was dramatically below birth weight even at two months of age, had been starving since birth.

not suck and swallow. She had a history of having seen a few doctors who told the mother that (1) the formula needed changing, (2) she had parasites, and (3) she needed an operation. Though given three opinions, no doctor had examined this child!!! This was common among Mexican doctors. Interview and prescribe. For this child, I calculated the calories she needed, provided a twenty cc syringe to do the feedings, and my wife and I taught her how to draw up the formula and drop it in the baby's mouth. We gave the mother a chart to keep track of the number of feedings, stools, vomiting episodes, and urinations. We hope we see her Wednesday. I have never seen such a malnourished child. The mother had eight other healthy children — at age thirty-five.

Wednesday, November 20

We went to the clinic today. I saw the baby with malnutrition. She hadn't gained any weight but her hydration was better. She had increased her urine output and stool output. She was vomiting more after receiving 400+ cc of formula. I found a heart murmur today and an enlarged liver. I wonder if she had high output failure or a congenital heart problem. I did not feel an "olive" though the vomiting started at the right time for pyloric stenosis.[4] It is hard to know if any of these things could be true. There are no tests available. Tuesday we may bring the baby to Tepic (the closest Mexican city) to a big hospital. I hope something improves with the baby by Monday!

The baby's history told exactly why she had become malnourished. The mother had been separated from the baby to have her gall bladder removed a few weeks before I started seeing her. During that time in the hospital, the mother's milk dried up. The baby never got used to a bottle and the mother couldn't always afford formula. She only saw family practitioners that did not know, or think, of other options for feeding the baby. In the U.S., the baby likely would have been hospitalized and fed by different means, including with an intravenous line and through a nose tube. When the girl returned home, doctors would have suggested that the mother use eye-droppers to continue her feeding before progressing to a bottle. But in this area of rural Mexico, none of these were an option. Instead, the family practitioners continued to push nursing and bottle-feeding.

4. Pyloric stenosis is a blockage of the small intestine that can occur at around two months of age. In babies with this condition, there is often an olive-shaped lump in the baby's abdomen. Usually an ultrasound can easily discover the problem.

The story continued after we had a weekend off in Puerto Vallarta. During the weekend I wondered how our little malnourished baby was doing. As we went back to our world of bank machines, American Express, and shopping for Christmas gifts, this mother struggled to feed a five-pound, one-ounce baby who was truly struggling for her life. My thoughts were really with her.

Monday, November 25

Back at the clinic, the great news is that, although the poor baby remains at five pounds, one ounce, she looks fabulous. Drooling, crying, more alert, sucking on her hand. All the doctors and staff were thrilled to see the look on the baby's face. One staff member even told me "Wow, you came down for three weeks and you saved a life." The story of this baby is the real story of our trip. It isn't enough to see the poverty, the broken streets, broken walls, broken windshields, TVs on luxury buses, luxury hotels, the tourists, and the indigenous people peddling their wares. The contrasts and paradoxes are thought provoking, but the story that stirred our hearts and feelings was the story of this baby with no name. She is called "Recently born." Many babies are not named here until they are baptized.

They aren't baptized until they are big enough. So many kids aren't named until they prove they are going to make it. How many babies die with no names? I don't know.

That baby's story was the most dramatic. But other stories revealed a lot about the culture and our experience there. One sixteen-year-old boy came in with gonorrhea that he had caught from a local prostitute. Prostitution is legal in that area, and boys are encouraged to use a prostitute for their "first time."

We saw many cases as "house calls" in the community where we were staying. I wrote in my journal about one of those house calls.

Wednesday, November 20

I have frequently seen patients in the town where we are staying rather than at the clinic. They come to our housing area at all hours. I have seen kids with colds, teens with cuts from their machete work, and everyone's ear infections. One time it was about nine P.M. when one of the leaders asked me to see a patient. A woman had come and asked for our help. Both her son and husband had high fevers. My wife and I walked with the woman on the dark dirt and rock road with our path lit only by flashlights. This was my first visit to a home in the town where we were staying. The woman was extremely poor, spoke poorly, and may have had a mental condition, according to the town leaders.

Her home was behind a restaurant on the beach. The floor was a mixture of dirt and sand. It was terribly uneven. Their beds were basically hammocks made of various sizes of cloth. The home had only one room with a doorway closed with a rag. To the right was a kitchen with a sink without plumbing. There was no bathroom visible, though I believe there was one in the restaurant. A few metal shelves had little on them. The husband and son were wrapped in lots of clothes. The husband never showed himself beyond being a lump of cloth in the larger bed. Did his Latin machismo forbid him the indignity of being examined? The sixteen-year-old son didn't mind being seen. He was obviously feeling awful. He had *dolor de la cabeza* and *dolor de la garganta* (headache and sore throat). His throat was red and he was extremely hot to touch. Based on his red throat, I treated both him and his father with antibiotics. Without testing available, I had to assume they had strep throat. I treated the father based on the history given by his wife. He didn't let me examine him. Who knows if he will be angry with her just for bringing us there? I don't know where I do more medical work— at the clinic or in the town where we're staying.

We had a meeting on the last day of our stay. The last entry of my journal reads:

Wednesday, November 27

Goodbyes:
We had a meeting today and everyone gave feedback. To a person, the feedback was positive both for Spanish classes and for the clinical experience. People were very emotional. Many of the volunteers got very close. One was crying with her farewell. She had to leave right after the meeting. The clinic medical director gave a very warm talk after the goodbyes about living here and about getting things done with different people from different places contributing. It was interesting because the philosophy seems to be: live, smile, and get along with people, and with common energy things will slowly and surely improve. It's not necessarily the most efficient way, but efficiency is secondary to living and getting along and getting by.

Tomorrow is Thanksgiving. Today I am thankful for this experience. I am especially thankful for Anna Cecilia Bermudez — the little girl formerly known as "Recently born." She looks better, is sucking more, seems more alert and is further from death. This has been an important experience for everyone here but very much an essential part of my experience. By simply pushing calories into her through syringe-feeding despite her vomiting, the baby has begun to thrive. I last saw the mother with a smile on her face. We brought her clothes for all of her nine kids and brought her new baby back from near death.

Many people have recognized that we saved a life on our three-week visit here. It is hard to put that down in words without it looking like hyperbole. But seeing the Mexican medical way of treating based solely on history, makes me believe the baby wouldn't have gotten the basic calories she needed. Instead she would have gotten more and more treatments such as "sweet water and tea."

It is pure coincidence that our paths crossed now. I am happy that I touched this life, and I am awed by how this life touched me!

This experience in words: fantastic,

scary, amazing, eye-opening, sweet, peaceful, slow-paced, many-layered, exotic, simple, beautiful, natural beauty, wonderful people, poverty, warm hearts, celebrations, fiestas.

About a year later the clinic's medical director sent me a picture of Anna Bermudez standing next to her mother with a dress on. She looked great.

50

A SCARY FEVER

Fevers.

It is the most talked about subject between pediatricians and families. Simply put, families fear fevers. Usually fevers help the body fight infection and serve as a warning that something is wrong. In the first few months of life, all fevers are serious. After that time, the real question becomes "Okay, there is a fever, but what is going on with the child?" It is usually the constellation of symptoms that gives you an idea of what is really happening. Sore throats, earaches, stomach pain, diarrhea — those are the common issues.

Most fevers — even high ones — are caused by viruses, which don't require treatment because the body defeats them on its own. Only a small percentage of fevers are caused by bacteria, which need to be treated with antibiotics. Nonetheless, it is hard to completely reassure a mother about her child's fever until the fever is gone. Until then, the child needs to be watched closely by the parent and, if necessary, followed by a pediatrician.

After managing thousands and thousands of kids with fevers in twenty-plus years of pediatrics, one child sticks in my mind. For several days, this seven-year-old boy had fevers over 102 degrees. He had few other symptoms except for feeling lousy and "looking ill." "Looking ill" is a subjective judgment that pediatricians have to make many times a month.

Only with experience can you acquire the skill to know the look in a sick child's eye that tells you their fever shouldn't be ignored. Such was the case with my seven-year-old friend. I knew his family because they lived in my town. I had been seeing both children in the family since they were born. I could tell by the look in the mother's eyes that she was worried too. I did some tests, but by the usual standards they were pretty normal. One test indicated some internal swelling that was invisible to the naked eye, but this was so non-specific that I could do little more than watch and wait.

I hoped it was a virus and would go away after seven to ten days. Usually when we get ill with a fever, the fevers come and go for several days and then stop. In this boy's case, two and then three weeks went by, and still the fevers remained. The ill look in the boy's eyes hadn't changed. It was time for more tests. I sent the boy down for some tests at Children's Hospital in Boston, where I was on staff. One of my colleagues there asked if I wouldn't mind getting the opinion of an oncologist — a cancer specialist. I recognized that leukemia was a possibility, but my previous tests had revealed his white blood cell count was low. All the children with leukemia whom I had seen during my residency had their illnesses discovered because their white blood cell counts were high. Leukemia is a cancer where the white blood cells multiply and begin to take over the bone marrow.

We sent the boy to an oncologist, who suggested a bone marrow test. The results were conclusive: positive for leukemia. Fortunately, the boy had not had it long and his prognosis was very good. The night after the diagnosis, I sat with the family at the hospital and witnessed their tears and shed a few of my own. I am sure the three weeks of fever were interminable for them. I am also sure their worst fears were realized when they learned their son had leukemia.

In reality, three weeks is a short time from their first visit to the doctor to diagnosis, especially for a tricky case of leukemia such as that one. The longer a child has leukemia before it is diagnosed and treatment is begun, the more difficult it is to treat. I feel better knowing I kept the door open for them to keep coming back. By close telephone contact and my respect for the mother's concern, we were able to discover the illness before it dragged on even further.

I always keep this story in mind in my practice. The biggest concern I have is that I would dismiss a parent's concern over a potentially serious problem. This story helps me remember not to. Pediatricians have to reassure a lot of families over fevers, but it's important to keep listening, so we do hear the call of the ones that need closer attention.

51

GUATEMALA:
A RAINBOW OF CULTURES

A year after the three-week program in Mexico, I went to Guatemala to study at a more intense language school. I wanted to improve my language skills so I could work better with Hispanic patients and do more volunteer work. I chose a program in Antigua, the ancient earthquake-ruined former capital.

The town is in a beautiful setting, nestled in the mountains and facing volcanoes. It is filled with Spanish-style red-tiled stone buildings. Antigua, which is not to be confused with the Caribbean resort island of the same name, is an academic center, with dozens of Spanish-language schools. I chose one of the oldest, a school that works with the many indigenous groups in the towns around Antigua to preserve their native languages.

My wife and our three kids came with me, and we

all attended the language school. The program was great. For three weeks, I had a very intense one-on-one tutorial entirely in Spanish. My family had the same for two weeks. My three-year-old-was in a day-care program she talks about to this day. "When I was in Guatemala . . ." she says. People laugh when they hear a nine-year-old talking about her experience in Guatemala.

On weekends, we traveled to different areas of Guatemala on trips arranged by the school. We traveled to Lake Atitlan, a glistening crater lake, and to Tikal, a wonderful tropical rainforest with Mayan ruins. One day we were taken to a nearby village, where the local indigenous people recounted their courting and wedding rituals. All these were great experiences for us, especially for the kids.

I kept a journal on the trip, as I usually do. I wrote a lot of my impressions in quick, bulleted notes. As I read it again now, I am hit with a wave of memories. It actually upsets me that I have allowed myself to put aside these important issues in my mind. My first entry covers poverty and hardship not known in our country.

My first impression of Guatemala was that it was a poor country. People in the cities seemed less poor, but their definition of "poor" was different than ours. We would consider many of them poor by our standards, but they would not consider themselves poor at all. The conversations I had with my Spanish instructor illustrate what I mean.

Her daughter was born with an abnormal heart. She had a common congenital heart defect called a ventricular septal defect, in which the wall between the ventricular chambers doesn't close as it should, before birth. The baby needed an operation to repair it, but she had to wait for a year and a half before her family could afford to have it done. Bandages, supplies, and food are not covered by the state-operated health system in Guatemala.

When the little girl finally went in for surgery, my instructor was in a different hospital having her second baby prematurely. Her husband wasn't there for his daughter's surgery because a few months before he had crossed through Mexico and into Texas to find work to pay for the surgery and hospitalization. He found a job in Houston. Eventually he came home, their daughter recovered, and they paid their bills. But what hardship they went through!

When I met her, my instructor had a good job and her husband was back working in Guatemala. They were happy. They weren't poor by these standards, especially in spirit. But we in the U.S. don't know this level of need. How often does a father in the U.S. have to migrate to another country to pay for surgery for his daughter?

After hearing my instructor's story, I told her I was interested in volunteering in a clinic while in Guatemala. Before I could get any further, she told me about her husband's younger sibling. When they were kids, the sibling was admitted to the hospital by American "doctors."

The family was later told that the child had died, but the body was never returned. It was later discovered that illegal adoption services from the U.S. had arranged for babies to be stolen from Guatemalan hospitals. The same story was repeated to me by others at the school about their families' experiences. They told me that American doctors are not trusted in Guatemala because of the history of illegal adoption rings. Obviously, volunteering was not going to be part of the trip for me.

I did have a medical experience, however. Midway through the second week I got a bug bite on my elbow. It wasn't much at first, but the swelling grew so much that I could not extend my elbow. Eventually, it had swollen up to the size of a softball and I couldn't lean on it. I had bought some Keflex, an antibiotic for skin infections, at the pharmacy in Antigua. (Keflex is only available by prescription in the U.S., but is sold over the counter in some countries.) After two days on Keflex I felt worse. I felt feverish, light-headed, and sleepy. I told my instructor that I needed the afternoon off. As I went to bed, the school's leaders came to where I was staying and insisted on bringing me to a doctor. Feeling terrible and not knowing which crazy infection I might have from the bugs in Guatemala, I agreed to go.

They brought me to a clinic, where I met with a very respectable and smart internal medicine doctor. He changed my antibiotic, and chatted with me about the state of medicine in Guatemala. He said the public health system was run by the government, and that a more exclusive private medical system was available for the wealthy. He said the public system was okay —

most kids were vaccinated — but supplies and access to treatment varied depending on where you lived.

The private system was for the people who could afford insurance. It only operated in the major cities where a practice could be supported. I was treated by, and educated about, the Guatemalan health system at the same time. I also educated my new doctor friend about our health care system. He was not aware that our health system in the U.S. was tiered by income as well.

In the end, his antibiotic worked, and I was better within twenty-four hours. The swelling in my grape-fruit-sized elbow went down and after several days I went back to show the doctor. He was happy at my recovery, and I thanked him and his staff for their help. Before leaving I mentioned my desire to volunteer and he graciously reiterated what I already knew about the reputation of American doctors in Guatemala.

A Fascinating Cultural Study

With volunteering out of the question, our intense Spanish language-learning became the main, but not only, focus of our trip. Guatemala is a fascinating cultural study, made up of hundreds of native peoples who continue to speak their own languages. When the Spanish conquered the Mayans, they did not wipe out the indigenous peoples as they had in other lands. They did, however, institute some rules for the natives. One was a requirement that they dress in a way that identified them. This led to the many colorfully woven garments for different groups of indigenous people that you see today in Guatemala.

My family and I were fortunate to travel to areas that allowed us to witness some of the issues faced by these indigenous cultures in Guatemala.

The language school arranged for a small group of us Americans to visit a community nearby called San Antonio de Agua Caliente, which means "St. Anthony of the warm water." The community opened themselves up to show us their traditions. We saw some women making their traditional blouses called "huipols" (pronounced "weep-eels"). They made us a traditional meal with tortillas. We were allowed to help, and they even let us try to make the tortillas ourselves by hand. The women made the hard work look easy as they clapped their hands rapidly to flatten out a ball of dough into a perfectly round tortilla before placing it on the grill. We failed miserably at the same chore.

One elder woman told us about their traditions. She told us that eighty years ago a man could grab a piece of cloth called a "tela" off the shoulder of a woman. In doing so the man said, "Tonight you will be my wife," and the woman had to comply. Today there are still courting rituals, but they have changed in the last eighty years.

I wrote in my journal what we learned about the group's courting traditions:

Today, after six to nine months of dating,

a woman's parents would talk to the man's parents to tell them it was time to get married. Then there would be a series of meetings. First, the elders would meet together. They would discuss arrangements for the wedding. Then a second meeting would include the bride and groom and witnesses to go over the agreements made in the first meeting. Then the two families get together with guests and have an engagement party. The father's side of the family brings gifts including thread for the woman to make her future mother-in-law a new huipol. In return, the mother-in-law makes the new bride a whole new outfit that she wears on her wedding day and thereafter. These gifts are woven, and take almost a year to complete. During that year, the bride and groom cannot be alone together. They were always seen in the company of younger siblings and cousins. When the wedding night comes, the witnesses give their statements of the "commitments" made. These commitments include, among other things, a list of gifts each family agreed to give each other. The gifts are exchanged. Then, on her wedding night, the bride is sent to the kitchen to keep food coming for the guests for five days of festivities.

We were amazed at traditions such as this one. And to think that each indigenous group had their own variations on all of the traditions. That meant Guatemala was a country of hundreds of cultures and traditions. The government takes advantage of this rich diversity to encourage tourism. Every tourism advertisement prominently features indigenous people and their intricate, hand-woven materials. Although today the indigenous diversity is used for the country's benefit, in the past the government tried to eliminate most of the indigenous population. Much of that war was supported by the United States, and President Clinton issued an apology for the support during his second term.

The indigenous groups are largely unrepresented in Guatemala. It is a situation that mirrors the plight of Native Americans in the U.S. Their lands were often taken. They tend to be poor and lack basic resources in their communities, such as plumbing, refrigeration, electricity, gas, and telephones. They have traditionally made their living off the land, growing their own food, but they are being pushed aside as their land becomes valuable to big food, fruit, or coffee companies. When they have tried to fight for their rights, they have been killed.

We saw an impressive church and rectory in a town called Santiago. The image is still clear in my mind. We saw firsthand the site where death squads had shot a priest for his work with the poor. A nearby memorial to the priest verifies the story. Events like these are repeated throughout Guatemala and in other countries. It is very discouraging to think that these death squads had U.S. support and often used American-made weapons.

We saw many poor women and children during our visit. The children worked as hard as the adults, often carrying bricks, wood, or even another child on their backs. When you shook the woman's hands you could feel the years of labor in their palms. The people we met were warm, caring people. Why are they such objects of oppression? And why do we Americans participate?

This wasn't a medical education in the true sense, but it made a lasting contribution to my medical studies. First, improving my Spanish is important to me and my practice. As the Hispanic population in the U.S. continues to grow, communication with Spanish-speakers becomes more important. Second, seeing so many cultures in a country as small as Guatemala reminded me that there are many cultures here in the United States. Tolerance and understanding of these diverse cultures and their traditions are essential to an empathetic practice of medicine. And third, the poverty in Guatemala — like that in Mexico and the Dominican Republic — is unjust. It is important for us all to recognize and acknowledge the economic injustices here and abroad and understand how we Americans unknowingly contribute to it. Nowhere was this clearer to me more than during my trip to Honduras the following year.

52

HURRICANE DEVASTATION
IN HONDURAS

The year after participating in the program in Guatemala, I went back to Central America to volunteer for two weeks. I joined a medical team working in Honduras to provide relief work a year after Hurricane Mitch. We would be visiting small towns in areas where indigenous peoples lived to deliver medical care and hear about relief efforts. The team needed a pediatrician, and I was available.

Even as I looked at the medical turmoil in the U.S., the troubles in Honduras, where the entire meager infrastructure was wiped out by a single storm, were at an entirely different level. I viewed the trip as a chance to do some meaningful service while further developing my Spanish language skills.

My trip was sponsored by Witness for Peace, a nonprofit organization. The medical team organized for the trip consisted of doctors and medical students whose specialties ranged from internal medicine to the emergency room, and from family practice to pediatrics. The doctors were bright and intelligent and cared about what they were doing. We discussed and debated all aspects of the trip: How much good were we doing? Were there better ways to set up our clinic? Would we have a more lasting effect if we did more teaching? Were we there for them or for us?

The trip started with a meeting in Los Angeles, where we learned the history of the organization. Witness for Peace was formed to witness what was happening in troubled areas of the world. The group's focus was on human rights. After Hurricane Mitch devastated Honduras, Witness for Peace organized our group to evaluate the country's medical condition.

How badly devastated was Honduras after Mitch hit in 1998? Among countries in the Western hemisphere, Honduras shot from thirteenth to second in the number of people living in poverty. Only Haiti had more people in poverty. Hurricane Mitch killed over 6,000 people in Honduras and hurt 12,000 more. It damaged sixty percent of the roads and half of the country's crops.

I was part of the third medical team sent by Witness for Peace. Our task was to provide medical services and report back on the devastation. In our orientation we were told we would "take back more than we give."

We were taught about the indigenous people we would visit. Indigenous people make up only seven percent of the Honduran population. Ninety percent of the country's population is of mixed Spanish and indigenous ancestry, a mix known as "Mestizo." In Honduras, unlike Guatemala, most indigenous groups were eliminated during the Spanish conquest. The unjust treatment continues today in Honduras. Two weeks before our trip, an indigenous man was shot by government police with a rubber bullet for peacefully protesting Columbus Day, which commemorates the Spanish conquest. At the same demonstration, police beat other protesters. During our trip, we would meet people who had witnessed the brutality.

After our orientation in Los Angeles we flew overnight to Honduras, arriving in San Salvador exhausted and sleep-deprived. From there we flew to Tegucigalpa, Honduras.

During the landing in Tegucigalpa, I was surprised that the first signs I saw along the road were for McDonald's, Burger King, and Pizza Hut. As it turned out, these signs were telling of the relationship between Honduras and American businesses. Everywhere I went in Honduras, even in the most remote villages on the border with El Salvador, I saw signs, trucks, and stores for McDonald's, Burger King, Pizza Hut, Little Caesar's, Quaker State, Coke, Pepsi, Marlboro, TGI Fridays, Dockers, Texaco, Mobil, and many others. I also passed the largest military base in Central America, a U.S. army base from which we had fought the forces in Nicaragua and El Salvador during the Cold War. The base had great facilities on flat land, a valuable commodity in such a mountainous country. It stretched for miles and even included well-groomed baseball fields. The presence of the United States of America was imprinted in one way or another everywhere we went.

Yet wherever we were, medicines, food, and farmland were in short supply for indigenous people. The predicament worsened after Hurricane Mitch. We learned from talking with people that all the relief efforts went to roads and major companies such as United Fruit Co., which lost banana trees in the storm, and needed roads to ship their goods. Subsistence farmers who grew their own food on mountain slopes — the poorest land — were heavily affected by the storm yet received no aid from the Honduran government or other governments.

On a Hillside over Tegus

After learning about the country and its troubles, I felt that we needed to get to work and help. Our first clinic was on a hillside village looking over Tegucigalpa ("Tegus," as the locals say). During Hurricane Mitch, part of the village had slid off the mountainside and buried hundreds of people. When we arrived, women were working hard to build retention walls, concrete steps, and drainage ditches so the tragedy would not be repeated. The women leaders were proud to show us their work. They had done all the masonry and heavy lifting of sand and concrete. The men of the village were conspicuously absent. Many of them had gone to find work on sugar or banana plantations or in clothing factories elsewhere in Honduras or as migrant farmers in the U.S.

In the village, you could still see a 100-yard strip of grass and brush where hundreds of people had been buried by mud. The strip of bushes where squatters' homes once stood is an inspiration for the communities and is left untouched out of respect for those who died in that spot.

After we held two daylong clinics near Tegus, we traveled close to the El Salvador border to an area of mostly indigenous residents. The residents had no services. No plumbing. No electricity. No phone service. Many had never seen a doctor in their lives. Houses were spread over miles of mountains and valleys, and residents walked as far as five miles to come see us. The residents learned of our visits on their battery-operated radios, the only means of mass communication in this remote region. Word spread quickly, and over a week of visits to tiny villages we would see as many as 300 patients each day.

Each day, we would travel to a village, receive a welcome from the local leaders, and then set up the clinic and pharmacy. At day's end, we would reverse the process, pack everything again, and go back to the town where we were staying in a dormitory operated by Catholic Relief Services.

The cases we saw stay vivid in my mind. We saw many common issues, some in very large numbers. Ear infections, asthma, parasites, and impetigo — a skin infection exacerbated by a lack of clean water — were far more common than in the United States. I wrote in my journal about the most heartbreaking cases. Here's a particularly poignant entry:

> I had to talk to a woman about her grandchild. She had brought the girl to us to evaluate her talking and learning. She was an eleven-year-old girl who was supposedly at second-grade level. The small girl repeated few words and sat with her mouth open and tongue hanging out. She had a prominent jaw and unusual features. She probably had a genetic syndrome and seemed mentally retarded. Though a full evaluation was tough to carry out, we had to tell this young grandmother that this child was unlikely to learn fully. We tried to have her understand that teaching her basic hygiene and protecting her as she reaches adolescence were priorities. I went to the pharmacy to get her vitamins (to at least give her something) and almost cried as I stood there. This grandmother came to us thinking we could help change her granddaughter. Her expectations were too high.

In the mountains near the border with El Salvador, we saw a number of patients with cleft palate. There seemed to be a high percentage of this abnormality, and the people told us they were seeing it more and more.

They suspected it was due to waste the U.S. military had buried nearby, but they couldn't prove it.

One day we saw a child with a huge head. She was six months old and her head measured fifty-four centimeters. A normal head at that age is between forty-four and forty-eight centimeters. The soft spot on her head, which is called the fontanel, was wide open, and the line where her skull plates connect, which is called the suture, showed a gap between the plates.

This meant there was a build-up of pressure inside her head. Such pressure is usually caused by water build-up, a condition called hydrocephalus. It's a correctable problem, but if left uncorrected it can be devastating as the brain tissue is pressed against the skull from inside.

The mother had been told that she needed to take her daughter to Tegucigalpa, the capital, for an operation. She was afraid to go because she feared "having a hole" put into her baby's head. She also couldn't afford it. The operation was free, but expenses such as transportation, food, bandages, and lodging were not. We raised money within our group to allow her to make the trip and get the operation. As the pediatrician in the group, my job was to persuade her to have the operation. After answering her questions and concerns, I convinced her no hole would be left visibly open in her daughter's head. We arranged for transportation to "Tegus," where the baby was taken to a hospital to have the operation.

On a daily basis we saw children who suffered from malnutrition. Many kids looked much younger than they actually were. That was especially true with the malnourished children. We saw malnourished infants, toddlers, and children. Age didn't matter. Seeing the malnourished babies was the hardest. One six-month-old child looked like he was two months old. He was pale with cold hands and a swollen face and belly, and he had a rash on his legs and in his diaper area.

We calculated how many bottles of formula that he needed. He would need ten, three-ounce bottles of Alimentum per day. We provided the Alimentum, which had been donated to us for the trip. After the Alimentum was gone we suggested milk supplemented with corn powder. We never knew the outcome with the little boy or any of the kids we treated. Maybe our suggestions worked. Or, maybe after the Alimentum was gone, the starvation came back to haunt the little boy. Usually we had some confidence that the community would help to support the starving children. We tried to make sure the community leaders knew who needed the most help. In Honduras it truly takes a village to raise a child.

Serious Cases

In dealing with the malnutrition we became frustrated in seeing such poorly directed relief aid. One day, after working in a clinic and treating several starving kids, we opened a closet and found cornmeal and rice that had been donated by USAID, a foreign aid agency of the U.S. government. The bags looked like bags of concrete and had the words RICE and CORNMEAL written in

English on the side. People in the community needed this food, yet because it hadn't come with clear directions on how to use it, and because the local leaders were never taught what to do with it, the food was never used. Instead it was trapped in a little-used closet while local residents went hungry. It was a sad statement. We, of course, redirected the food to the families who needed it, and gave them information about what was in the bags and how to use it.

The cases we saw showed the lack of accessible health care. Some of the adults we saw had clubfeet. Clubfoot is a condition in which the foot is severely turned inward so that the person is forced to walk on the side of their foot. In the U.S., clubfoot is easily corrected with a brace in the first year of life. But in this village, grown men whose clubfeet had never been treated were forced by their condition to walk on the side of their feet. That side grew to be calloused like the heel of anyone else's foot.

We saw kids with untreated cardiac defects. I remember one, a fragile seven-year-old girl, whose chest wall vibrated with a murmur at every heartbeat. A murmur is a rushing sound of blood in the heart indicating a turbulent flow. When examining a heart there are ways to grade a murmur. Grade I is barely audible. Grade II is when you can hear it most times the heart beats. Grade III is easily audible. With Grade IV the murmur starts to have a "thrill," or vibration. Grade V has a thrill that you can feel. Grade VI is so loud the stethoscope doesn't even have to touch the chest for you to hear it. This poor girl had a grade VI murmur that sounded like a harsh rumble. It was the worst murmur I have heard in twenty-two years of pediatric practice. Yet the mother had brought her to me to see if we could do something about her size. She had no idea that her daughter had a heart valve problem that would kill her if not corrected. The girl needed to go to Tegucigalpa and perhaps to the U.S. to have her heart fixed. Talking to the mother about this was not easy at all.

The wife of the town's leader brought her son to me because the boy didn't seem very strong. We had seen the mother earlier in the day, when she served us lunch at her home. Many times in the town where we worked the town leaders had us check their family and friends. It was often a political favor even though they may not have been the ones most in need of our services. We always complied, though we resented being used in that way. We felt it was more important to care for those in need than it was to further the town leader's political career.

This time, however, seeing the town leader's son wasn't just a courtesy. The child had Down's syndrome. After I explained the diagnosis to the mother, she confessed she knew something was wrong. She was unaware of Down's syndrome and its implications. One of the problems children with Down's syndrome can have is a heart defect called a ventricular septal defect. It's a condition where the wall between the major chambers in the heart doesn't fuse together before birth. This leads to backward flow toward the lungs and a shortage of blood around the body. It usually needs to be repaired if it is large enough to cause this backward flow.

The six-month-old with Down's syndrome had a significant heart defect in need of correction. He had a very loud murmur indicating the ventricular septal defect. I talked to the mother about Down's syndrome children, and told her I hoped the cardiac repair would be simple. I told her I believed God put Down's syndrome children on Earth to show us what happiness was, since so many of them show their joy freely. The mother told me she had great faith in God, and she hoped God would be with her. We did, too. We sent her to the capital to see a surgeon for her son.

In another town, a woman brought her fifteen-month-old son to me. She wanted me to make him better. He couldn't hold his head up, arched his back regularly, would not hold his gaze on anything, and could only suck and swallow liquids. At the time I saw him he felt feverish and sounded congested in his lungs, but that was not the problem his mother wanted fixed. The boy had cerebral palsy, a condition in which brain damage causes children to lose control of their muscles. The boy's cerebral palsy had likely been caused by a severe infection, possibly meningitis, that had gone untreated at two months of age. He would never be able to care for himself. His cerebral palsy was so severe that he would be prone to pneumonias and would most likely die from pneumonia before he was twelve. In the U.S., we would work to prevent that through operations and special feeding arrangements. In the U.S., the boy would have had preventive surgeries and plenty of care to insure good health and growth.

As I tried to explain some aspects of his health, the

mother held him across her lap in a manner demonstrating total love. A friend on our team translated for me, since my Spanish was not good enough to communicate everything I needed to. I watched the mothers' eyes as we spoke. We told her about the infection, the cerebral palsy, the chronic care needed, and the risk of pneumonia. Her eyes stayed attentive but unemotional for a time. My friend asked her how she felt about all of it, and in seconds her eyes filled and tears flowed. I watched them stream down her face. We held her. We gave her antibiotics for the baby's pneumonia and enough for a couple of future ones, and we asked what else we could do.

"Could you pray with me?" she asked.

We prayed together in a small circle. Afterward, we escorted her out to the path for her walk home. Then my friend and I went behind the church and cried again together. It was so hard to tell these parents something so devastating that would require such dedicated work from them. They came expecting our help. Certainly, some of their expectations were set too high. Perhaps they had heard about American doctors. There are probably stories about children who go to the U.S. for surgery or other treatments. It is hard enough in the U.S. to tell a parent that there is nothing to do, but at least there are more services to help them. Here I was forced to send a mother out the door with her child diagnosed with cerebral palsy to walk miles back home, the child in her arms and only antibiotics and vitamins in her pocket.

The level of medical need in Honduras was enormous at the time I saw these disheartening cases. While I was there, I couldn't help but be terribly bothered by the strong presence of American businesses and the simultaneous lack of American aid. In fact, I wondered how much we contributed to some of the problems. I couldn't help thinking how much Coca-Cola contributed to the number of dental cases we saw. Our companies were everywhere. Our army base sat on miles of prime farmland, while miles away locals farmed on steep mountainsides. The base was well-equipped, but for miles all around children were starving. And I know our companies are there reaping profits.

53

LESSONS FROM EL RANCHO SANTA FE

I have since returned several times to a very special place in Honduras. Amid the extreme poverty that continues to haunt Honduras is a refuge for children called El Rancho Santa Fe, about forty miles north of Tegucigalpa. It is an orphanage for children who have lost their parents, and it is run by the organization Nuestros Pequenos Hermanos — Our Little Brothers and Sisters.[5] What makes the place so special is the love, joy, caring, and sharing that comes from these orphaned children and those around them.

The orphanage takes its "El Rancho" name from the horses and cows living on the farm. El Rancho Santa Fe is set up according to the philosophy that these children have suffered one great loss in their lives, so

5. www.nphhonduras.org.

the orphanage will not let them have another. No child is given up for adoption. They can have faith that the orphanage is their home. They come to the orphanage and are accepted into a family of 600 children. The orphanage is run by Honduran staff and foreign volunteers. It takes children from a period of abandonment to a life of love.

The children are the story of this orphanage. Every function is meant to improve their lives. The kids have clean homes, clothes, good food, a school, and access to health care. They are kept safe, and they are taught a work ethic to help them value their contribution to society. Even six- and seven-year-olds sweep and clean without complaint because they see around them a community where everyone contributes.

The children are alive. Their eyes sparkle with joy when they take your hand. They want to know your name and want you to know theirs. You are immediately accepted into their community. You cannot avoid being drawn into their life by the affection they show.

They are thriving at this place. Many of the children complete high school, and they all learn a trade. Many go on to university, and two from the orphanage are currently in medical school. Such a success rate cannot be matched in many American communities, much less in other impoverished Honduran communities.

I have volunteered three times at El Rancho Santa Fe, but my contributions pale in comparison to what I have received from these orphans. The lessons are many, but the most obvious is that when children are given clothes, food, housing, a safe environment, health care, and education, they thrive. Of course they need love and care, but when provided with those basic needs by loving people they find the love they need and share it.

Each time I leave El Rancho Santa Fe, I leave with sadness because of the love I feel there. Every visit brings momentous sentimental memories that I cherish. I wish more people could experience it and learn the lessons about contributing to a greater social good. At El Rancho Santa Fe, everybody working there is working for the benefit of the children. That frame of mind is much needed in our society. When people work hard and focus their efforts on a greater social good, they can change society for the better. That's a useful lesson we in the U.S. should keep in mind as we work to repair our health care system.

54

HUMOR IS BETTER THAN NOVOCAINE

You have to laugh. People are funny. We are all funny. People need to laugh with each other. It is important for all of us to recognize our funny side.

It connects us as humans.

It lifts our spirits.

It joins us together like no serious conversation can.

It improves our memory of each other.

Which do you remember more: a funny time together or a serious time together? Most of our memories are fun, happy times or sad, emotional times — the extremes of our emotions. Even when you meet someone momentarily, if you share a laugh it helps you remember each other. Humor, and laughing specifically, is good for your health. Humor is the best medicine.

I remember a patient I saw only once. He was seventy-five years old. The only reason he was seeing a pediatrician was because I was good at suturing. On the day he came in, the internal medicine office next door had nobody working who knew how to suture, so they called and asked if I would come over and help. Their only other option was to send the man to the emergency room, which they didn't want to do.

When I went into the internal medicine office, the old gentleman gave me a toothless smile. He had cut himself while cutting a bagel. His index finger had an inch and a half gash along its side. He was laughing at his own clumsiness.

I reassured him that bagel injuries were common, and we kept chatting. He recalled other times he had received stitches, mostly during his military service. I told him I had learned to suture in the military and had gained lots of experience doing it during my own service time.

As we talked, I began preparing his finger. I set out my syringe, forceps, needles, and suture. Then I drew up the Lidocaine, a numbing medicine, into a syringe.

"I won't be needing that, Doc," he said, motioning toward the needle and syringe. I'd heard that before but I preferred using it rather than having my patients jump and squirm when the needle went in. Then he explained.

"One time I was going to the bathroom and my

daughter came running to see me," he said. "I didn't want her to see me, so I hurried to finish and went too fast with the zipper. I caught my pecker in the zipper. I needed eight stitches, but they said I couldn't get the Novocaine down there. So they had to sew me up with nothing. Ever since, if I could get stitches down there with no numbing medicine, I figure I can get stitches anywhere without it. So go ahead and just sew me up. I'll be fine."

So I did. I chucked the needle and syringe to the side and went right to sewing his finger back together. We laughed about his story and he continued with others. Most of them were war stories about him and his friends. He never flinched or jumped while I worked. Occasionally he shook with laughter as we both chuckled.

When I was finished, he didn't even realize I was done. He had just finished another funny story when he realized that I was facing him and listening.

"Oh, you're done," he said.

I bade him farewell, offering him advice for cutting bagels in the future. He said he'd be careful or else he would look me up again.

I never saw him again, but my spirits lift every time I think of him. He was living proof that laughter is the best (numbing) medicine.

I don't know what's going to happen in the world of medicine in which I practice. We have so much to work on — the push for the max, the lawsuit mentality, the millions of people without insurance, dissatisfied patients, unhappy doctors. All I know for sure is that patients who make me laugh and lift my spirits give me the drive to continue practicing in a difficult world. I watch and wait for our medical world to be more supportive of the kind of practice that promotes these connections between doctors and their patients.

55

WHAT MAKES IT
ALL WORTHWHILE

I once participated in a conference on cross-cultural health care. It's an area in which I've developed a strong interest because I have practiced in many countries and plan on doing more work in Latin America. The premise of the conference was that doctors face cultural issues in daily practice, and with the growing diversity in our country, clinicians need to understand their patients' cultural background in order to improve patient-doctor interaction. The idea was that our patients will be more likely to follow our instructions if we understand their cultural perspectives, and adapt our care accordingly. Understanding their cultures will also help us build dedicated patient followings for our practices.

At one point during the conference, a group of clinicians shared experiences with patients who had helped them overcome cultural and religious barriers, leading to some very close patient-doctor relationships. Some stories were so touching they brought tears to many participants' eyes. On the way out of the conference room, an acquaintance told me it was a wonderful reminder of why we had gone into medicine. "We don't get reminders of that very much anymore," she said. "These experiences make it all worthwhile."

Yes, it is the relationships we develop that make this business of medicine worthwhile. The conference led me to recall some of my patients and the experiences with them that had been so bonding.

I thought about some of the notes that patients had written me over the years. It is not unusual that several times a year I would receive a note from a parent about how my care had affected their child. A note I recently received was from the mother of a three-year-old boy.

The boy was petrified when I first saw him. He had asthma, and coming to the doctor's office was so stressful that it was hard to help him. Examining him was a heart-wrenching ordeal. He screamed in fear. When I started seeing him, I immediately tried to befriend him. I brought my shaving kit of toys into the exam room, and without looking at him, I would start playing with the toys. I wouldn't focus on him until he joined me in play. At first it took a while, but he began to join me in play more quickly with each visit. Eventually he got used to me examining him as we engaged in play. After treating his asthma over several months, he was in much better control of the disease.

His mother wrote me a letter of thanks:

Thank you so much for being such a friend to our son. He loves going to the doctor's now. Before he would cry as soon as we saw the building. Now he asks me, "Can we go see my doctor, Mommy?"

I remember another child with a chronic neurologic condition. I had been caring for him and his mother for two years when she sent me this note:

I want to thank you for everything you do for us on a continuous basis. Even though my son's situation is very sad, you always bring a silver lining to it. Your genuine concern for him and my family is clear to see. Thank you. Many people's concern fades after the initial discovery of illness while it is still very forefront for the family. You realize that, and remain sincere in your concern. I could never thank you enough for your extreme professionalism and humanity.

Another mother appreciated the way I tried to ease her daughter's fear by "examining" her doll first. The mother wrote:

I just wanted to let you know how much I appreciate the quality of care that you have given to our daughter. When you "examined" her baby yesterday, I wished that I had brought a video recorder with which to capture such a sincere act of compassion. Thank you so much for all that you do.

These letters fill me with joy and make me feel that my efforts are worth it. They demonstrate the deep connections that I have made with these families — connections that touch their hearts and mine. These connections are what makes practicing medicine worthwhile.

Was this taught to me in medical school? Did I miss that class? Here I am more than twenty years out of medical school — seven years in the Navy and more than fourteen years in private practice. Maybe I should have known this. But now I discover an essential truth of practicing medicine.

AFTERWORD

Between the writing of this book and its publication, health care in America has worsened. We've had two presidential campaigns in which the number of uninsured in America debated by politicians rose from 40 million to 44 million people. Practice life has gotten tougher for doctors because of rising costs, and many doctors have seen their incomes stagnate. Malpractice insurance has climbed by over 50 percent per year in many places, and rising malpractice rates have caused OB-GYN offices to close in some states. Other overhead costs for small practices such as heat, medical malpractice insurance, required technology upgrades, and medical insurance for employees have increased as well. It appears that more closures may come, especially for small group practices.

Smaller hospitals continue to be weeded out of the

system. As a result, emergency rooms at larger hospitals suffer from overcrowding. Many emergency rooms lose money because rising insurance costs and decreased access to Medicaid/Medicare have forced many people to seek free ER care instead of visiting a doctor's office.

Pharmaceutical prices continue to rise to astronomical levels, while the quality of medicines has come under intense scrutiny. Medicines making fortunes for pharmaceutical companies have been pulled from the market, leaving some stocks teetering and patients wondering what to do.

Some families seek drugs from Canada while others face bankruptcy due to medical costs. These families may face an even harder time when a new federal bankruptcy law takes full effect.

Doctors are pushing to keep their salaries at the same levels as previous years. Meanwhile, doctors and their patients are unhappy with a system in decline.

But I don't feel discouraged. I am hopeful that in years to come, Americans will see that our health care system is the biggest problem facing our government. The claims from insurers, pharmaceutical companies, and high-tech companies that the system is working (for them) will fall on deaf ears as Americans face a system where only the wealthy and the extremely poor are served.

I'm hopeful that we will be able to make important changes in our health care system. Insurers should be required to offer very low-cost alternatives for their subscribers, possibly by offering plans with less expensive drugs and less access to high-tech medicine.

Lawmakers should pass a "Good Samaritan in Practice" law that would reduce frivolous lawsuits against doctors and encourage greater doctor-patient relationships. Pharmaceutical companies should be made to stop advertising high-cost medicines, and go back to marketing through doctors like they used to. Curbs should be implemented to cut back on the overused technical side of medicine.

Patients, for their part, need to expect less than what they perceive to be the best medicine, because high-quality medicine can be delivered at a lower cost, even if people think the most expensive medicine is the best.

I don't have all the answers. But, at the very least, we need to ask more broad questions about all the areas of the U.S. health care system, and then we need to have the courage to take dramatic steps to bring about effective solutions.

We can have a world where doctors practice caringly without fear of malpractice. Where patients feel a closer connection to and dedication from their doctor. Where drug prices are controlled so everyone can get the medicines they need. Where a greater variety of insurance options guarantee everyone coverage and nobody has to go to the emergency room for free care.

After all these years of practicing medicine, I'm still learning things. But I do know what I want. I want to make connections. I want to serve patients like family in a town with several cultures. I want to use my language skills to gain better ties with Spanish-speaking families. I want to play with kids until they enjoy coming to me for exams. I want to help new mothers. I want to get new parents through those first few months, and then those first few years.

I want to work hard to care for families in a small community. I hope my practice doesn't have to struggle too much to get the payments it earns from insurers. I want to volunteer each year for a short time in countries like El Salvador or Honduras. And before my practice days wind down, I want to leave U.S. medicine and practice for a longer time in a country where health care needs are more severe than here.

In the meantime, I hope and pray someone is smart enough to preserve the integrity of the sacred doctor-patient relationship. I pray our system doesn't implode under the weight of technology costs and pharmaceutical costs. I pray doctors aren't driven to see more and more patients. I pray patients can learn to trust their doctors again.

And I hope ten years from now I'll still be able to see that child waiting for me and give her the time she deserves.